Companion to the Lectionary

5. All Together for Worship

Stewart,

With best wishes from
your colleagues in
Corporate P+O.

October '95.

Peter Sheasby

Companion to the Lectionary

5. All Together for Worship

EPWORTH PRESS

0 7162 0495 9

*First published 1994
by Epworth Press
1 Central Buildings Westminster
London SW1H 9NH*

Second Impression

*Typeset by Regent Typesetting, London
Printed and bound in Great Britain by
Mackays of Chatham PLC, Chatham, Kent*

Contents

Contributors

Keith Burrow
Sandra Clack
Christine Odell
Colin Ride
Peter Sheasby
Graham Slater

Preface

To follow in your wife's footsteps is always a daunting task. To be asked to edit this volume in the Epworth Lectionary series was therefore both an honour and a challenge. Only now do I fully appreciate what it took for my wife Christine (Odell) to write all the prayers in Volume 4 – and I have written less than a quarter of this one.

I am indebted to my co-writers, Christine Odell, Colin Ride, Sandra Clack and Keith Burrow, for the considerable effort they have put into producing this material. I am grateful for the interest they have shown in this project, together with all the advice, support and encouragement that they have offered to me. I would also like to thank Kathryn Schofield and Michael Townsend for sharing their wisdom with us in the early stages. We have had the benefit of much thought and time from members of the Epworth Press editorial committee, and particular mention must be made of Graham Slater for his helpful comments on the work.

Behind each of us there have been many other people who have given their continual love and support to us in all that we have been doing. Many have said that they look forward to seeing this volume in print, and I can only hope and pray that everyone's faith in us has been justified by the book in front of you now.

Halifax, July 1993   Peter Sheasby

Introduction

All-age Worship

As promoted in recent years 'All-age Worship' has not been welcomed universally. In part this is because it has been seen as blurring the edges between worship and learning and challenging the assumption that adults worship God while children learn about Jesus. In part it is because many preachers (ordained and lay) do not find it easy to relate to an all-age congregation, especially to its youngest members. If I did not come from a Western Protestant tradition I do not believe that I would find as much resistance to the very suggestion that everyone – young, middle-aged and the more senior – can truly worship together.

When to use this book

Churches have been gradually integrating all ages into their worship for many years. I grew up in the tradition of morning Sunday Schools, where the children join the adult congregation for the first few minutes of the morning service before they depart for their own activities; and of the monthly 'Family and Parade' service, that much maligned attempt to satisfy the needs of the whole congregation. This book can be used in the preparation of such services. It is also for those churches who have struggled to renew their worship life by looking again at the true meaning of worship and discovering that all ages can share their faith together for the benefit of each other and most importantly to the glory of God. I am tempted to say that this volume is for those who *do* think worship should be enjoyable and uplifting to everyone, regardless of age, but who don't feel they have the experience and language to lead such a service.

Who can use this book

If this book is to be used in an act of worship, the material it contains will need to be prepared carefully and prayerfully. It cannot just be picked up and taken into the pulpit. But it contains ideas and prayers which should help worship leaders from all traditions to broaden their range of resources. It is based on years C and D of the JLG2 Lectionary, but, with use of the indexes, could be utilized by those who use the ASB (JLG1), Common Lectionary, or no lectionary at all. We have related what is written to the lections set for each Sunday, drawing out a possible central theme.

What is in this book

Each Sunday contains a **Presentation** which offers suggestions for a theme, how to use and present the readings, and ideas for drama, discussion, games, visual aids, etc. to help the congregation latch on to the theme and direction of that week's worship. This is usually followed by a **Call to Worship** and then a range of **Prayers** (Adoration, Confession, Intercession, Offering etc.) emerging from the readings. Other material such as **Meditations** are also included. Most Sundays are concluded with a **Blessing** or **Dismissal**.

The worship leader must decide what is suitable for the needs of a particular service. Sometimes preachers will choose their theme and see if this book is helpful to them, at other times it might lead their thoughts and suggest a theme for preaching. How much of the material is used will depend upon the church's practice but it is suitable for all ages and is not necessarily for use only when all ages are present together.

Also see the section 'How to use this book'.

How to use this book

As a rule:

– words in Roman type are to be said
– words in *italics* are instructions
– words in **bold** type are for congregational participation.

Responses within prayers can be simply introduced or printed on the church noticesheet. There are some prayers where the words are not a straightforward repetition of a phrase and in such cases the whole prayer can be copied (for single occasion use see copyright note at the front of the book). If this is not possible or desired either two voices can be used or the whole prayer read by the worship leader alone. The 'thought for the week ahead', or sometimes the opening or closing words, could also perhaps be included on the church notice sheet.

In Advent and Lent where there are suggestions which follow on from those for previous Sundays, a discussion between worship leaders would be helpful. Churches can also take up the suggestions for themselves and encourage those designated to lead worship to use them.

All material has been prepared using the Revised English Bible.

Material for Year C

9th Sunday before Christmas

Presentation

God's parental love for the world is known through both its initial creation and its continuing nurture. We find God not only as we wonder that creation exists, but also as we wonder at its order, mystery and beauty. The use of pictures to illustrate the Bible readings would be helpful, as would the use of suitable music before or after them.

The passage from Job can be read effectively by alternating male and female voices.

Call to Worship

Let us, with all creation,
Shout in joy and praise:
God made us, loves us, saves us!
Blessed be the name of the Lord!

Prayer of Adoration

From nothingness, from chaos,
you called forth existence,
order and life:
L: With all that is, and was, and will be:
R: **Creator God, we praise you**.

From darkness
you called forth light;
from swirling waters,
stable, dry land:
L: With all that is, and was, and will be:
R: **Creator God, we praise you**.

From the fullness of your heart
and the riches of your imagination
you filled the world
with all varieties of life:
L: With all that is, and was, and will be:
R: **Creator God, we praise you**.

From your desire to love
you fashioned woman and man
to seek and to know you.
L: With all that is, and was, and will be:
R: **Creator God, we praise you**.

Your love for all that exists
is the beating heart of creation;
the pulse of life that is never stilled.
You continually protect us, guide us and strengthen us,
never forgetting one thing you have made:
L: With all that is, and was, and will be:
R: **Creator God, we praise you**.

In the name of Christ, the Word of God.　　**Amen**

Prayer of Confession

Loving Father God,
　　you never forget us, but we often forget you.
Loving Mother God,
　　your love is strong and constant, but ours is
　　weak and fitful.
Author of the universe,
　　you gave yourself to us in the gift of Christ,
　　but we hold back much of ourselves from you.
Continue your creative work within our lives.
Forgive us, heal us, make us new.
In Jesus' name.　　**Amen**

Offering Prayer

Generous God, giver of life itself,
in response to your creative love, we offer to you
our money, our talents, our lives, ourselves,
to be used in the shaping and reshaping of the world.
in the name of Christ, our Pattern and our Saviour.　　**Amen**

Blessing

The God of new beginnings sends you out into the world.
Creation is your home. Go – live, love and be joyful
In the name of the Father, the Son and the Holy Spirit.
Amen

8th Sunday before Christmas

Presentation

Humankind proves unable to resist turning away from God, the Author of all life. But God has promised we shall not be destroyed, and Christ is the fulfilment of that promise.

Illustrate the Genesis reading with a picture of a rainbow or dance with coloured ribbons. Luke can be mimed.

Call to Worship

Come to our God, for he gives
   light to dark lives:
   hope to the despairing;
   forgiveness to the sinful;
   love to each one of us.
God of life, we worship you!

Prayer of Praise

Lord, we praise you
   for the colour that you bring to our lives,
   lives that would be grey and dismal without you:
   the fiery hues of the love that burns within our hearts;
   the cool blues and greens of creation
   that refresh our souls;
   the deep, dark colours that remind us
   that even in the darkness you are there.
Lord, we praise you
for the colour that you bring to our lives.   **Amen**

Prayer of Confession

Creator God, we ask forgiveness for the sins of the human race, which destroy the balance and variety of your creation. We have polluted, exploited, been careless with your gifts.
Creator, forgive us.   *Silence*

We ask forgiveness for the sins of the nations, which lead to wars, injustice and hunger. We have been greedy, hated those

different from ourselves and been indifferent to the sufferings of
others.
Creator, forgive us.   *Silence*

We ask forgiveness for the sins of the church, called to be a light
to the world but often God's weak and unwilling witness. We
have been apathetic, inward-looking and lacking in the
confidence of faith.
Creator, forgive us.   *Silence*

We ask forgiveness for our many sins, that lead to our
unhappiness and the unhappiness of those around us. We have
been selfish, insensitive and afraid of the demands of love.
Creator, forgive us.   *Silence*

In the name of the man who has brought and brings us
forgiveness, Jesus Christ our Saviour Lord.   **Amen**

Prayer of Thanksgiving

We thank you, Ruler of the Universe,
for the many signs of hope we see within your creation:
for rain that brings life to dry and dusty land,
wild flowers that cover spoil heaps and ruins
and the healing of broken relationships between peoples and
nations, between ourselves and others.
L: God of hope: R: **We thank you**.

For rivers that run clean once more,
impoverished land reclaimed and made fertile,
and the healing of broken human lives,
of bodies, minds and spirits.
L: God of hope: R: **We thank you**.

For the coming of hope into the world with the birth of a child,
his life, his death and his rising from the tomb,
for the gifts of your son, Jesus Christ, the Word of life.
L: God of hope: R: **We thank you.**   **Amen**

Dismissal

Go out into the world as living signs of hope,
To love, serve and worship, in the name of the risen Lord.

5

7th Sunday before Christmas

Presentation

God can use the most unlikely situations and people for the purpose of healing creation. We are God's people not because of who or what we are, but through trust.

The Genesis passage may be read by several voices.

Call to Worship

To each one of us,
God calls, saying
  'Come, my child,
  trust in me
  and I shall be
  your rock and your saviour.'
Let us worship in faith
our strong and loving God.

Meditation

Lord, how Sarah laughed
at your promise that her old, barren body
would conceive, carry and give birth;
that her wrinkled, tired arms
would nurse and comfort a fresh-faced child.
She laughed, yet your promise was fulfilled
in the surprising gift of Isaac, her son.

Lord, how they laughed and scoffed
to see the promised Messiah, the King of the Jews,
nailed up like a 'low-life' killer or thief;
the popular hero condemned to death
by the populace he had loved and healed.
They laughed, afraid of such love,
love stronger than death itself.

Lord, how they laughed
to see a once powerful and wealthy church
now peopled only by impoverished old women,
who said that they 'kept the faith alive'.
They laughed, but now that enfeebled church

flourishes, grows strong in you.

Lord, how I laughed, and wept, with joy
to learn that the unbelieving, the powerless, the scoffer
are all alike understood and loved by you;
and that even I, inadequate, sinful, blind,
am your child, whom you call and cherish,
you – the mighty, perfect, all-seeing God.

Prayers of Intercession

We, the people of God, drawn from every nation,
pray for the peoples and nations of the world,
and for their leaders.
We pray for . . .
L: The Lord hears our prayer: R: **Thanks be to God**.

We, the people of faith, hearing God's call,
pray for the church, both here in . . .
and throughout the world, and for its leaders.
We pray for . . .
L: The Lord hears our prayer: R: **Thanks be to God**.

We, the people of hope, heirs to God's promise to Abraham,
pray for those who live in need of hope;
the sick, the anxious, the depressed, the destitute.
We pray for . . .
L: The Lord hears our prayer: R: **Thanks be to God**.

Faithful God, Abraham heard your promise and believed.
His whole life was shaped by his trust in you.
May we, the children of Abraham, stay faithful to you by leading
lives that radiate hopeful love.
In the name of our loving brother, who remained faithful to you
until death itself, Jesus Christ our Lord.   **Amen**

Dismissal

Go out into the world in confidence and faith,
for the faithful creator of the world goes with you.

6th Sunday before Christmas

Presentation

God, the great I AM, is the God of the living, of every new generation. The God of abundant life rescues us from slavery, calling us to live by love, not by mere obedience.

Act, mime or dance the Exodus passage, using a representation of the burning bush.

Use two voices to read from Luke.

Call to Worship

Come, let us worship the living God,
the God of yesterday and tomorrow,
the God who makes the present moment holy
and sets us, his people, free.

Prayer of Adoration

God of mystery and power,
    your greatness is beyond our understanding.
    your glory blinds us
    and we step back from the fire of your love.
God of mystery and power,
    we worship and adore you.

God of Abraham, Isaac and Jacob,
    you come to us, the living God of every time,
    calling us and challenging us
    and giving us the courage to live new lives.
God of Abraham, Isaac and Jacob,
    we worship and adore you.

God of goodness and mercy,
    you re-create us in your image, from the inside out,
    cleansing our souls and lives from sin
    and writing the law of love upon our hearts.
God of goodness and mercy,
    we worship and adore you.   **Amen**

Prayers of Intercession

Voice 1:   O God, I cry to you for freedom.
I am the man put in jail for attempting to right an injustice.
I am the woman in the grip of torture for holding on to my religious beliefs.
I am the boy slaving in a sweatshop to provide cheap exports to the West.

L: 'Let my people go' says the Lord:

R: **Lord, help us to set the captives free**.

Voice 2:   O God, I cry to you for freedom.
I am the woman enslaved by hunger, spending my strength in the struggle for existence.
I am the man carrying the burden of watching my children die, one by one, from the diseases of malnutrition.
I am the small girl, held captive by fear, as warfare rages around me.

L: 'Let my people go' says the Lord:

R: **Lord, help us to set the captives free**.

Voice 3:   O God, I cry to you for freedom.
I am the man whom no one really knows, living out my last days in lonely isolation.
I am the woman held in the iron bands of grief with no one to hear my cries for help.
I am the child who is different from other children, imprisoned by that difference.

L: 'Let my people go' says the Lord:

R: **Lord, help us to set the captives free**.

L: Lord, we each cry to you for freedom: freedom from our limitations and weaknesses; freedom from fear, from sin and guilt and death. Lord, hear the cries of all your people and set the captives free, for the sake of your son, Jesus Christ, who was led captive to the cross that we might know glorious liberty.   **Amen**

5th Sunday before Christmas

II Sam. 5.1–5
I Cor. 15.20–28
Luke 25.35–43

Presentation

'Kingship' implies power, wealth and glory. But biblical kingship is seen in the context of a covenant with God and the people. God is the 'king of kings' and the king of Israel is a shepherd king, tending his nation. Jesus, the good shepherd king, lays down his life for the sheep, thus revealing his true majesty.

Display symbols of royalty – crown, sceptre and orb – alongside a crown of thorns, crook and globe.

Call to Worship

The Lord is king.
King of the universe.
King of our hearts.
Come, let us offer to our God
the homage of worship and praise.

Prayer of Praise and Thanksgiving

The world is a place of great beauty and wonders:
    of mighty snow-capped mountains
    and microscopic organisms;
    of jewelled hummingbirds, brilliant butterflies
    and stately, lumbering elephants.
Let us praise God for the rich variety of creation:
L: For the majesty of your creation, King of the Universe:
R: **We give you thanks and praise**.

The world is a place where love abounds:
    the love of man and woman, parent and child;
    the love of family and friends;
    the love that finds expression
    in caring, holding, comforting, forgiving.
Let us praise God for loving relationships:
L: For the majesty of love, King of the Universe:
R: **We give you thanks and praise**.

The world is a place polluted by sin:
    sin cutting us off from God, one another, creation itself;
    sin poisoning us, our relationships, the earth around us.
    Empty of all but love, Christ the King was born among us,
    giving himself to cleanse us and make us one with God.
Let us praise God for the gift of his Son:
L: For the majesty of Jesus Christ, King of the Universe:
R: **We give you thanks and praise**. **Amen**.

Prayer of Confession

Almighty God, you have given us power,
power over ourselves and other people.
But we have not used that power responsibly.
We have lacked self-control and hurt those we love.
God of power, forgive us.

Creator God, you have given us wealth,
a home, food, clothes and many possessions.
But we have not used our wealth responsibly.
We have been poor stewards, keeping too much for ourselves.
God of all that is, forgive us.

All-knowing God, you have given us wisdom,
knowledge and a way of seeing things that is all our own.
But we have not used our wisdom responsibly.
We have failed to share our thoughts and resisted new ideas.
God of wisdom, forgive us. **Amen**

Offering Prayer

Lord of all, accept these gifts – for they are yours.
Accept our service – our lives are yours.
Accept us – for we are yours,
Followers of Christ the King. **Amen**

Dismissal

You are members of God's royal family:
Go out, robed in the glory of Christ
with the crown of self-giving upon your heads
and show the majesty of his love within your lives.

4th Sunday before Christmas
Advent 1

Jer. 33.14–16
James 5.1–11
Luke 21.25–36

Presentation

Instead of (or as well as) an Advent candle wreath, use another means of counting down to Christmas: perhaps a large Advent Calendar (five windows with appropriate pictures behind) or a single large candle marked off into five sections.

The readings today and in the coming weeks contain a number of references to trees. (e.g. Jer. 33.15, Luke 21.29). A 'family tree' for Jesus could be 'grown' during the coming weeks. Starting with God as the trunk, the prophets (today Jeremiah) as the main branches, Elizabeth/John and Mary as the highest branch leading to Jesus, then on to the disciples and eventually to us.

Call to Worship   *If there is a Christmas tree*
The evergreen Christmas tree reminds us
   of God's everlasting love.
We praise God, for all good things received in the past,
   enjoyed in the present and promised for the future.

Prayer of Praise

We prepare to celebrate, once again, the birth of Jesus,
a baby born 2,000 years ago, who changes lives today.
We praise you, Father God,
– for the gift of your Son, Jesus Christ;
– for the Word, who existed before the world was created;
– for the promise of his coming again in glory.
We seek your forgiveness,
– for the times when we have forgotten to praise you;
– for the ways in which we have disobeyed your Word;
– for turning our backs on your love and serving only
   ourselves.

During this time of Advent,
   fill us with joy, so that we may be ready to worship you;
   fill us with hope, so that we may be ready to find you;
   fill us with love, so that we may be ready to serve you.   **Amen**

Prayer of Petition

When will your day come, Lord?

All around us there is war, conflict between nations, fighting
amongst factions, hatred between individuals.
When will you bring peace?

There are good things in our world, but we are still surrounded
by cruelty and greed, gossip and jealousy, ruthlessness and
deception.
When will your kingdom fully come?

We are encouraged by those who work for justice and peace but,
as crisis follows crisis, we are overwhelmed by the scale of human
suffering, from warfare and persecution, famine and drought.
How can we hope for a better time ahead?

Lord,
   give us your peace in our hearts
      and the strength to be peace-makers;
   give us your hope in our hearts
      and the patience that springs from confidence in you;
   give us your love in our hearts
      and a concern for others that never ends.
In your Son, we saw peace, hope and love born in the world,
your presence alive and at work.
May you work in us and through us, today and for ever.   **Amen**

Final word, a thought for the week ahead

You must be patient and stout-hearted,
for the coming of the Lord is near.   *(James 5.8)*

Dismissal prayer

L: Creator of the universe: R: **Give us life**.
L: Saviour of all: R: **Give us peace**.
L: Holy Spirit: R: **Fill our hearts**.
L: Eternal God: R: **Be with us, now and for ever.**

                       Amen

3rd Sunday before Christmas
Advent 2

Isa. 55.1–11
Rom. 15.4–13
Luke 4.14–21

Presentation

*If the 'family tree' is being used, add Isaiah and Paul (Romans 15.12
– explain that a 'scion' means a 'grafted branch'). Think about
learning. Paul says, 'The scriptures written long ago were all written
for our instruction.' How do we use the Bible? What have the
scriptures to say to us today? Look particularly at what Paul says
about 'the encouragement they give us'. The Bible is not a list of do's
and don'ts; it is a support when we need help.*

*The Luke reading lends itself to dramatization. Either make up a
scroll or use a big Bible for the reading, and have one voice read the
narration and another the words of Jesus. Leave a silence for the
words to sink in – it would have gone quiet in the synagogue!*

Call to Worship (*Rom. 15.6*)

We delight in singing, we enjoy the sound of the organ.
With one mind and one voice we praise the God and Father of
our Lord Jesus Christ.

Prayer of Confession   *Introduce by reading Isa. 55.7*

Lord, you know how hard it is always to do what is right.
   A word of criticism, a gesture of dismissal, a look of disgust, an
   exclamation of pride – they just slip out and sometimes we
   don't even notice what's happened.

Lord, you know how hard it is always to know what is right.
   Sometimes we have to decide in haste or under pressure;
   sometimes we misread a situation and, when we realize our
   mistake, it is too late to change.

But we don't want to be evil or to choose what is wrong, and
there is no need that we should.
And so, confessing our sins,
we pray for forgiveness and for guidance.
You understand us better than we understand ourselves,
and you love us, despite our faults and failures.

Strengthen our desire to love and serve you,
following in your way and obeying your commandments.
We thank you that you freely forgive.
Help us to go and sin no more.   **Amen**

Prayer for understanding   *Based on Isa 55; could follow reading*
Great God,
we cannot hope fully to comprehend you,
for your ways are higher than our ways,
your thoughts above our thoughts.
Your words give comfort when we are sad,
encouragement when we are disheartened,
inspiration when we are empty of ideas,
instruction when we need to learn,
and for this we thank you.
Help us to read, note and understand
all that is written for us in the Bible and,
accepting your forgiveness and trusting in your love,
to find true life.   **Amen**

Offering Prayer (*Luke 4.18, 19*)
With the Spirit of the Lord,
may these gifts be used to announce good news to the poor, to
proclaim release to the prisoners and recovery of sight for the
blind; to let the victims go free, to proclaim the year of the
Lord's favour.   **Amen**

Final Word, a thought for the week ahead

May God, who is the ground of hope, fill you with all joy and
peace as you lead the life of faith until, by the power of the Holy
Spirit, you overflow with hope. (*Rom. 15.13*)

Dismissal

L: Peace of God: R: **Calm our fears**.
L: Hope of God: R: **Lead us on**.
L: Joy of God: R: **Fill our mouths with praise.   Amen**

2nd Sunday before Christmas
Advent 3

Presentation

Zephaniah was a prophet when the Jews had once more been dominated by another nation. Sometimes we too feel overwhelmed by the things which hold us back from living our lives freely for God. Zephaniah's words brought hope to the Jews. They also speak at all times to those who long for a better future.

Add Zephaniah to the prophets on the 'family tree', and Zechariah, Elizabeth and John alongside the central branch representing Mary and Jesus.

Call to Worship

We know that, sometimes to our surprise,
God can speak to us in our worship.
Let us, then, not only sing our praises, but also
listen for words of comfort and challenge today.

Prayer of Praise

'Rejoice, rejoice with all your heart'.
Lord, this is your command to us and, recalling the joys of life, it is easy to obey.

Yet it is often difficult to express our joy;
– the beauty of a newborn baby leaves us lost for words;
– the sight of mountains against a clear blue sky
  takes our breath away;
– a tender kiss from a long-lost friend brings a lump in
  our throats;
– a moment in which we are aware of your holy presence
  fills us with silent wonder.

We rejoice in our hearts;
  we rejoice that you have set us in such a beautiful world;
  we rejoice that your never-failing love is always with us;
  we rejoice that you came to us in Jesus, the living
    expression of your grace;
  we rejoice that, through him, we are made whole.

May we never stop thanking you
   for all the sources of our joy.   **Amen**

Prayer for Forgiveness

As we meet in church today, as we worship you, our God,
we are like Zechariah worshipping in the holy place.
We come week by week but not always seeking anything
different or new.
Forgive us for our complacent attitudes and feeble expectation.
Speak to us clearly and help us to believe.
May we, like John, be filled with your Holy Spirit.
Send us out to tell people about Jesus and bring reconciliation to
your broken world.   **Amen**

Offering Prayer

We give thanks for all we have:
   homes and food and clothes, and money to buy them.
Lord, with these gifts,
   we offer ourselves and all that is ours to be used
   according to your love and in your service.   **Amen**

Final Word, a thought for the week ahead

May God, the God of peace, make you holy through and
through, and keep you sound in spirit, soul and body, free of any
fault when our Lord Jesus Christ comes.   (*I Thess. 5.23*)

Responsive Dismissal

L: Go, holy people: R: **We go with God.**
L: Go, peaceful people: R: **We go with God.**
L: Go, loving people: R: **We go with God.**
L: and God goes with you.   **Amen**

Sunday next before Christmas
Advent 4

Presentation

We are familiar with Mary's great song of joy to God but we don't always listen closely to the words. Using an overhead projector or large sheet of paper write up the Magnificat, line by line, and alongside it write a modern paraphrase. Or look up a paraphrase and use it to help people understand what Mary meant. Make up a prayer based on the Magnificat or use the one below.

Mary should be added to the 'family tree', towards the top of the main trunk and leaving room for Jesus to be added on Christmas Day.

Call to Worship

People of God, young in body, young in mind, young in faith, remember Mary, mother of Jesus, and give thanks that you too have been called and chosen.

Prayer of Adoration

Mary speaks for us all. Make this prayer your own
God is great,
  I'm thrilled that God loves me and sets me free.
  I'm no one important, but God gives me everything I need.
  So much has been done for me.
God is holy,
  and all who believe know that God cares for them.
  We see God's strength in the downfall of proud people and
  foolish ideas, and in the poor people swapping places with the
  powerful.
God fills hungry people with good food,
  and rich people are sent away hungry.
  If I live serving God with my life I will not be forgotten,
God promised Abraham's children mercy,
  and that means that I am forgiven.
Praise God, for ever and ever.

Meditation – How can I?

How can I be a child of God?
    Lord, I am not good enough to be a member of your family.
    I am weak-willed, lazy in prayer, lacking in faith.
Why have you called me to be your follower?

How can I show people Jesus?
    I am not eloquent with words or skilled in the scriptures.
    I am shy, reserved in my words and restrained in my actions.
Why do you want me to be your disciple?

How can I receive your Spirit?
    I am not special, just a person struggling through life.
    I am ordinary, of no rank or standing in the world.
Why have you chosen me?

How can I know you?
    I am not wise or powerful or of royal birth.
    I am sinful, often ignoring you in my life.
Why me, Lord? What can I do?

Lord,
    if you want me to follow you, guide me;
    if you want me to speak in your name, inspire me;
    if you want me to show your love, love me;
    if you want me to worship you, fill me with your Spirit.
Lord, if this is what you want, I want it too.
So be it.

Final Word, a thought for the week ahead

By God's act you are in Christ Jesus; God has made him our
wisdom, and in him we have our righteousness, our holiness, our
liberation. Therefore, 'If anyone must boast, boast in the Lord.'
(*I Cor. 1 30–31*)

Dismissal

L: Christmas is coming: R: **We wait with expectation**.
L: Jesus is coming: R: **He is our Saviour**.
L: God is with us: R: **Praise God.   Amen**

Christmas Day

Micah 5.2–4
Titus 2.11–15
Luke 2.1–20

Presentation

*If a 'family tree' has been built up, then place the name of Jesus in a
prominent place at the top of the main trunk, the centre of the tree, but
leaving 'room for growth' – the disciples and the church. Instead of a
star (or fairy!) put a cross at the top of the Christmas tree.*

Call to Worship

Glory to God, in highest heaven
and on earth peace to all in whom God delights.
Happy Christmas! Christ has come!
Let us worship with joy and love.

Prayer of Thanksgiving

To God we pray:
For the joys of home: for gatherings of family and friends;
   for the young with their simplicity and enthusiasm;
   for parents with their responsibilities;
   for the elderly with all their happy memories.
L: For the joys of Christmas,
R: **We give you thanks and praise**.
For the joys of celebration; for all the greetings we have
   received; for friendships revived and renewed;
   for special food, decorations, bright lights;
   and for those around us who share our rejoicing.
L: For the joys of Christmas,
R: **We give you thanks and praise**.
For the gifts we have sent and received; for comforts and
   joys; above all for the gift to us of your Son, Jesus
   Christ, our Friend and Saviour; for his coming as a
   child to win our hearts; for his living and dying and
   rising; for the new life we find in him.
L: For the joys of Christmas,
R: **We give you thanks and praise**.
Loving God, your Son seems so small and vulnerable as he
   enters the world this Christmas, and yet we know that

people from all races have come to recognize him as
King of Kings and Lord of Lords. Accept the worship
and devotion that we offer. Use us to further the
kingdom of love which he came to establish.   **Amen**

Prayer of Wonder

From a tiny seed grows a tall fir tree.
Brought into a house and decorated with lights
and tinsel, it gives joy to all who see it.

From a tiny baby there came such love as had never been seen
before.
Lovingly held in his mother's arms,
he was worshipped by shepherds and kings.

From a small clan there came a king to rule over Israel.
Arrested as a trouble maker,
he was condemned to death on a cross.

From one man's death came salvation for the world.
If we turn to him, he offers forgiveness
and changes our lives.

Lord, as we remember Jesus, who came as a baby,
but grew to be the man who altered the whole of history
help us never to dismiss what seems small and insignificant but,
in all things great and small,
to express your eternal love for the world.   **Amen**

Final Word, a thought for the day

Jesus will grow up to lead his people with all the power of the
Lord. We are safe because God's greatness has reached all over
the world. Now peace can come.   (*Based on Micah 5.4*)

Responsive Dismissal

P: **Thank you God for your gift**:   L: Of peace with Jesus.
P: **Thank you God for your gift**:   L: Of joy with Jesus.
P: **Thank you God for your gift**:   L: Of love with Jesus.
Go in peace, joy and love and celebrate this day with all God's
children.   **Amen**

1st Sunday after Christmas

Presentation

*The gifts of the wise men suggest what is going to happen to Jesus.
While Christmas presents are still in mind talk about the gifts which
Jesus brought to us: love, joy, peace, salvation. These could be
represented by wrapped parcels containing a 'heart', family photo,
record of quiet music, life-saving ring, a cross etc.*

*Without preparation the Matthew story of the Wise Men could
easily be dramatized by asking members of the congregation to mime
the various parts as it is told.*

Call to Worship

We eat so much at this time that we can be, literally, 'fed up with
Christmas'! But we need to be nourished by other things, and not
least by the Word of God.

The feast of Christ is never finished,
always satisfying and a never-ending joy.
Let us worship God who feeds us with all that is good.

Prayer of Praise

L: Praise God who sent Jesus into the world:
R: **He has come to announce good news**.
Those who mourn will be comforted, those who are captive will
be set free, those who are sad will be joyful again.
L: Praise God who sent Jesus into the world:
R: **He has come to announce good news**.
Waste places will blossom again,
desolate cities will rise with new buildings,
robbery and crime will be replaced by justice.
L: Praise God who sent Jesus into the world:
R: **He has come to announce good news**.
We are the ministers of God, blessed by the Spirit.
L: Praise God who sent Jesus into the world:
R: **He has come to announce good news**.
We have heard and seen what Jesus has done. It is our task, with
the Spirit's help, to continue his work.

L: Praise God who sent Jesus into the world:
R: **And calls us to announce the good news of his coming.** **Amen**

Prayer of Confession and Intercession

Son of God, we confess the sins
   which separate us from you.
On the dark places of sin,
Light of the World, shine your forgiveness.

Lord, we confess there are still countries of the world at war,
   nation divided against nation.
On the dark places of hatred,
Light of the World, shine your peace.

Lord, we confess the faults within our church,
   which divide Christians, and weaken our outreach.
On the dark places of distrust,
Light of the World, shine your mediation.

Lord, we confess our lack of charity,
   which causes other people to suffer.
On the dark places of neglect,
Light of the World, shine your compassion.

Lord, we confess our need of the Light,
   who will illuminate for us the right path for life.
On the dark places of selfishness,
Light of the World, shine your selfless love. **Amen**

Offering Prayer

Loving God, treasure the gifts we offer.
Money for the work of the church, time for the needs of others
and love for all. **Amen**

Blessing

May Jesus bless you with all his gifts,
joy, peace, forgiveness and love, each given for you,
so that at the end you will feast in heaven. **Amen**

2nd Sunday after Christmas

Presentation

Each reading today is about serving God, and it is appropriate, at the beginning of a new year, to provide an opportunity for personal commitment.

At the offering, invite each member of the congregation to write their names on a piece of paper and to place it, with their money, on the collection plate. This can serve as a sign either of their first response to God's call or of their re-dedication. This will be especially helpful if there is no Covenant Service on this Sunday, or to introduce the meaning of the Covenant to children who may leave the service.

All the readings lend themselves to the use of several voices, either playing the chief participants in the episodes in I Samuel and Luke or listing the different gifts in Romans (12.6–8).

Call to Worship

God gave his Son to redeem the world.
Jesus gave his life to bring forgiveness.
The Spirit is given to all who follow the path to heaven.
In this worship we give ourselves to God, in praise and
adoration, in penitence and thanksgiving, in faith and obedience,
and in preparing ourselves for God's service.

Prayer of Praise

'I have seen with my own eyes', said Simeon.
  Lord, we worship the child
  who came to reveal you to the whole world.
  Glory to you in heaven and on earth,
  For you are a loving God.

'Thanks be to God', said Anna.
  Lord, we worship the child
  who came to save all humankind.
  Glory to you in heaven and on earth,
  For you are a forgiving God.

'God's favour was upon him', wrote Luke.
  We worship the child become man
  who lived a perfect life of teaching and healing.
  Glory to you in heaven and on earth,
  For you are a caring God.

Today, we respond, offering ourselves in his service.
  We worship Jesus
  who is the Lord of our lives.
  Glory to you in heaven and on earth,
  For you are a faithful God.

Glory to you in heaven and on earth, for you bring joy to our
hearts, wisdom to our minds and peace to our souls.
This is what you have done for all who know Jesus.
Thanks be to God.   **Amen**

Prayer   *To follow an act of self-offering*

Loving God,
we thank you that you welcome, with open arms, all who respond
to your gospel and fill them with your Spirit.
We ask your blessing on those for whom today is a time of
commitment or re-dedication.
May they find joy in your service.
We thank you, too, for all who use the gifts of your Spirit in the
life of your church: preachers, administrators, teachers,
counsellors, leaders, carers, and all who are generous, supportive
and loving.
May we, encouraged by their example, offer ourselves to you,
open to your transformation and eager to know your will. We ask
it in the name of Christ, our Lord.   **Amen**

Dismissal

We have heard that Christ has come.
Let us go in peace.
Blessing and honour and glory be yours,
our God, for ever and ever.   **Amen**

YEAR C

1st Sunday after Epiphany

Josh. 3.1–17
Acts 10.34–48a
Luke 3.15–22

Presentation

The Christmas decorations have now been put away, but the joy of Jesus' birth remains as John the Baptist announces his adult ministry, his proclamation of the good news in word and deed. Explore how and where the good news is shared today – referring to books, radio, television etc. and using a globe and missionary notes.

Call to Worship

God sent the word to the Israelites, gave the good news of peace through Jesus Christ, and speaks today where Christians worship him. Let us then hear God's word for us today as we worship in spirit and in truth.

Prayer of Thanksgiving *After the readings*

Thank you, Lord, for all who, through the ages,
have spoken your word.

We thank you for the patriarchs and prophets of Israel who
listened carefully to the Lord's voice and told the people what
they must do: for Moses, who gave the Law; for Joshua who
led them into the promised land; for Isaiah and Jeremiah who,
in times of difficulty, spoke words of encouragement and
comfort.
Thank you that, when we are in difficulty, your word still speaks
to our need.

We thank you for John the Baptist, imprisoned and eventually
killed for preaching against evil. He challenged people to
repent of their sin and pointed them towards Jesus,
proclaiming him as the one who would destroy evil in the fire
of the Holy Spirit.
Thank you that, through faith and baptism, we have received
forgiveness for our sins.

We thank you for Peter and the apostles who continued Jesus'
mission to the whole world. They travelled far and wide,
spreading your word and opening up the kingdom to Jews and
Gentiles, women and men, free persons and slaves.

Thank you that today, ministers, missionaries and preachers
continue that work in every country of the world.

We thank you for Jesus, the living Word. His words are the
foundations of our faith and everything we believe is based on
his truth. Words of judgment, words of hope, words of peace,
words of joy, words of love flowed from his lips and come to us
in the Bible. His words will live for ever.
Thank you that we have heard the gospel of Jesus, words for all
time. May we be able to tell others what we have
heard. **Amen**

Meditation – Standing up in faith

'Take your stand in the river', the Israelites were told.
Amid the flooding waters,
where the current is flowing fastest,
there we take our stand:
against the flow
which carries us so easily along;
against racism, against greed,
against violence, against evil.

'I now understand', said Peter.
God's wisdom is greater than ours,
and our minds must always be open to learn.
Jesus is for all, not just for the respectable,
the educated, the cultured, the well-to-do.
Open the door to the outcast, the poor,
the addict and the stranger.

'I am not worthy', said John.
Why us? What have we to give?
How can we say what is right or wrong?
How can we dare to speak in God's name?
The sin of the world is still around us
waiting for judgment, needing a challenge.
We don't need to wait for another to lead us –
in Christ we are worthy. Evil be gone!

2nd Sunday after Epiphany

Presentation

Moses was told he couldn't do it all himself. Who today helps God in acts of kindness, justice, evangelism or ministry? Take the opportunity to focus on one person or group of people who serve God – missionaries (abroad or at home), lay workers, deacons/ deaconesses, preachers. This could be in an act of thanksgiving for them, dedicating them in God's service or giving a challenge to join them.

The meditation would be best read by various voices.

Call to Worship

The Lord calls us to worship,
  we meet in God's house.
The Lord calls us to serve,
  we meet others in God's name.
The Lord calls us to salvation,
  we prepare to meet God in heaven.

Prayer of Confession   *A framework for prayer*

For ignoring the needs of others;
Lord: **Forgive us**.
For looking for reward and praise;
Lord: **Forgive us**.
For keeping power to ourselves;
Lord: **Forgive us**.
For ignoring our special gifts;
Lord: **Forgive us**.
For not listening to your call;
Lord: **Forgive us**.
For conforming to the world;
Lord: **Forgive us**.
We are sinners, we are not worthy to face Jesus.
Lord: **Forgive us**.
In mercy you hear us, in grace you respond,
with joy you receive us, with love you forgive.
Thank you for your endless patience and kindness.   **Amen**

Meditation – for all who serve Jesus

The load is heavy, Lord, and I am weak.
Disciple! I haven't the faith, I haven't the charisma.
Why should Jesus call me?
What am I, but a confused seeker after God?

The load is heavy, Lord, and I am weak.
Fisher! I haven't the patience, I haven't the ability.
How can I speak about Jesus?
What right have I to tell people about faith?

The load is heavy, Lord, and I am weak.
Preacher! I haven't the courage, I haven't the knowledge.
How can I share what I barely understand,
what I hardly live up to?

The load is heavy, Lord, and I am weak.
Follower! I haven't the time, I haven't the will.
Which way should I go?
How can I be sure I am on the right road?

The load is heavy, Lord, and I am weak.
My Master! You ignore my weakness, disregard my
imperfections.
You want me, even me, to be your servant.
I am chosen and called to go with you.

The load is heavy, Lord, and I am weak.
My Leader! With you I am strong, with you I am brave.
Give me any task you have for me,
for you carry my burdens and lighten my load.
With you I can, I will, I am.

Dismissal

Christ behind you, Christ before you,
Christ within you, Christ beside you,
Christ to comfort and to guide you.
Christ in hearts of all that love you.
Christ lead you in love to friend and stranger.   **Amen**

3rd Sunday after Epiphany

Presentation

'Waiting' sums up all three readings: the Israelites wait for the cloud to move on; Jesus, quoting Isaiah, explains how the Israelites' waiting has come to an end (even if they don't understand that); Paul writes that the Corinthians still wait expectantly for the final revelation of Jesus. Talk about: What people wait for today – news, visitors, holidays. How people wait – worriedly, expectantly, impatiently. Do we seek the guidance of God as we wait?

Call to Worship

L: The Lord is here: R: **The Spirit is with us**.

L: The Lord has guided
   us to this place: R: **Let us worship**.

L: The Lord speaks to us: R: **Let us listen to the Word**.

L: The Lord is with us: R: **Today, tomorrow and forever**.

Prayer of Adoration

Loving God, we praise you that throughout history you have been with your people and guided them in your ways.

We praise you for bringing the Israelites safely through
   the wilderness, guiding them with the pillars of cloud
   and fire.

We praise you for the life of Jesus, whose example we
   follow, and for his teaching which guides our thoughts
   and actions.

We praise you for the disciples and St Paul who continued
   to guide the church through difficult times and guide
   us still by their writings.

We praise you for the Spirit alive in the world today, who
   gives inspiration to those who seek to do your will.

We praise you for the Spirit alive in us. Guide us in our
   worship and service, so that all we say and do comes
   from you.

We praise you that you call us to share in the life of
   your Son Jesus, for you are a God always to be trusted.

Amen

Prayer of Intercession

Voice 1: The Spirit of the Lord is upon me because he has anointed me.

Leader: We pray for all who need the Spirit's help:
in their work, in their family life, in their sickness, in their life of faith.
Lord bless them and give them the support they need.

Voice 2: He has sent me to announce good news to the poor.

Leader: We pray for all who speak out in Jesus's name:
those who share the gospel – in worship, on the street corner, at work, with their neighbours.
Lord, inspire them and give them the right words to say.

Voice 3: He has sent me to proclaim release for the prisoners, recovery of sight for the blind; to let the broken victims go free.

Leader: We pray for all who serve others in God's name:
those who care for people in prison, in hospital, in the community, in . . . in this country and throughout the world.
Lord, strengthen them and give them your love.

Voice 4: He has sent me to proclaim the year of the Lord's favour.

Leader: We pray for all who seek the kingdom of God:
those who are strong in faith and know that you are with them in all they do; those who are weak and uncertain, still trying to discover your will for them.
Lord, fill us with your Spirit and help us in worship and service, to use the many gifts we have been given. **Amen**

Blessing

May God direct you with the guidance of the Spirit.
May God inspire you with the gift of wisdom.
May God bless you with the love of the Son. **Amen**

4th Sunday after Epiphany

Presentation

We need special places and special rituals to give focus and shape to our worship, but if we ourselves are not open to the living God, they can be empty of meaning.

Display pictures or models of different kinds of churches under the words 'We are the living temple of God.'

Call to Worship

We are the living temple of God,
a people set apart for praise.
Let us worship with joy and reverence
the God who is in our midst.

Prayer of Invocation   *Could be used responsively*

Lord, let your glory fill each one of us,
   let it fill this church,
   let it fill the world.

Lord, let your peace fill each one of us,
   let it fill this church,
   let it fill the world.

Lord, let your truth fill each one of us,
   let it fill this church,
   let it fill the world.

Lord, let your love fill each one of us,
   let it fill this church,
   let it fill the world.

Lord, let your praise fill each one of us,
   let it fill this church,
   let it fill the world. **Amen**

Meditation   *on the conversion of a chapel*

The glory of the Lord has departed from our chapel.
Rolls of carpet stand where once the mighty organ pipes
rehearsed the angels' song.
Rolls of carpet, of different widths and colours,
lie close together where once church members sat,
never touching.
Rolls of carpet of differing qualities
stand upright in the pulpit,
waiting for their design to be revealed.

The glory of the Lord has departed from our chapel.
But Albert, the naughtiest lad in the Primary,
has been heard to say,
as he guided an elderly lady, even older than himself,
to a remnant of very good Wilton,
that the glory of the Lord
has never departed from him.

Offering Prayer

Holy God,
like the widow with her two tiny coins,
we offer what we have to you,
our money, our love and our lives.
Consecrate them all, that we may be
a temple of beauty for our living God.

Prayer of Petition

Loving God, who called into being the church to be Christ's body
on earth, we ask that you give to all who seek to serve you the
gift of your Holy Spirit, that we may fulfill our calling with
courage, wisdom and compassion. Through Christ our head and
cornerstone.   **Amen**

Dismissal

God lives and moves about among us.
He is our God and we are his people.
Let us live and love and seek and serve,
that the world may become his glorious temple.

5th Sunday after Epiphany

Jer. 13.1–11
I Cor. 2.1–5
Luke 5.33–39

Presentation

God's word is a word of power. The word of the prophet not only foretold events but brought them to pass. The message of the gospel was powerful enough to convince and convert even on the lips of ineloquent preachers! The new understanding that Jesus brought was too explosive to be contained by old ways of thinking.

Ask the congregation to suggest words that have the power to change things, get things done (e.g. Stop it! Votes for women!)

Call to Worship   *Could be used responsively*

Come and worship as God's new and holy people,
recreated by his word of love.
Sing to the Lord a new song
and offer him your wonder and praise.

Prayer of Adoration

Creator God, who, by your word,
   brought the world to birth,
   we worship you.

Word of God, who, by giving yourself,
   became the human Word of life,
   we worship you.

Spirit of God, by whose power
   words sway, convince and save,
   we worship you.

God the first word,
God the last word,
God the word for us now,
   we worship you.   **Amen**

Prayer of Confession

Author of good,
We confess that we have not listened to your words.
Our ears have become deaf to your call:

– by listening to the clamorous voice
  of society, with its materialistic morals;
– by listening to the insistent demands
  of our own selfish wants and desires;
– by listening to the hubbub of our busy lives
  and never listening through it to hear you.
Forgive us. Open our ears. Speak to our hearts.
Guide our lives along the path of love.
In the name of Jesus, your word of forgiveness to us.   **Amen**

Prayers of Intercession

During these prayers there will be times of silence, of listening
for God's word. Let us pray:

Loving God, speak words of power to the nations.
Speak of justice, compassion, wisdom and peace:
Silence
L: Saving God, speak words of power:
R: **That we may turn and be healed**.

Loving God, speak words of power to your church.
Speak of faith, endurance, unity and service:
Silence
L: Saving God, speak words of power:
R: **That we may turn and be healed**.

Loving God, speak words of power to those who suffer.
Speak of comfort, healing, hope and resurrection:
Silence
L: Saving God, speak words of power:
R: **That we may turn and be healed**.

Loving God, speak words of power to each one of us.
Speak of forgiveness and acceptance, life and love:
Silence
L: Saving God, speak words of power:
R: **That we may turn and be healed**.
In the saving name of Christ our Lord.   **Amen**

6th Sunday after Epiphany

Presentation

God does not obey our rules – rules about what is wise or the correct thing to do. Love does not seek conformity, or the good opinion of others. It seeks to fulfil the real needs of human beings. It is living and dynamic, overflowing narrow constraints. Ask the congregation to name rules that govern daily life. Why were they made. Do they ever conflict with a Christian conscience?

Call to Worship

L: This is the day that the Lord has made:
R: **Let us rejoice and be glad in it**.
L: Let us give thanks to the Lord, for he is good:
R: **His mercy endures for ever**.

Prayer of Adoration

Immense and amazing God,
   your greatness bursts the bounds of our imagination,
   and fleeting glimpses of your glory
   leave us blinded by its brilliance.
Immense, amazing God, we worship you.

Holy and righteous God,
   your perfect goodness draws our faltering souls to you.
   The vision you give, of life in all its fullness,
   transforms our understanding of the world.
Holy, righteous God, we worship you.

Generous and loving God,
   your love for us fills our hearts to overflowing,
   and, burning up our selfishness and sin,
   breaks down the barriers between us.
Generous, loving God, we worship you. **Amen**

Prayers of Intercession

Voice 1: I am scared.
  scared of saying something stupid,
  scared of wearing the wrong clothes,
  scared of treading on someone's toes.
  I'm too scared to let them know and love me.

Voice 2: I am scared.
  scared of disobeying others,
  scared of breaking any rules,
  scared of thinking for myself.
  I'm too scared to put love first.

Voice 3: I am scared.
  scared of any change to my life,
  scared of losing myself,
  scared of loving someone too much.
  I'm too scared to let God in.

God of encouragement, we pray for those whose lives are
governed and shaped by fear, the fear that inhibits love and
stunts our spiritual growth.
  Spirit of freedom, liberate us;
  Spirit of truth, enlighten us;
  Spirit of love, make us bold;
that we may follow Christ our Saviour along the perfect way of
love. **Amen**

Offering Prayer

Generous God, teach us how to give. Teach us how to give of our
time, our possessions, ourselves. Our love can never measure up
to yours but we ask you to accept this offering as a pledge of
ourselves to you, in Jesus' Name. **Amen**

Dismissal and Blessing

You are God's free and joyful people.
Live according to the rule of love!
And may the blessing of God,
Three in One and One in Three,
fill all our lives for ever. **Amen**

9th Sunday before Easter

Presentation

By teaching in parables Jesus challenged his listeners to discover truths for themselves. This was the kind of education that draws the pupil out, creates a response. Proverbs warns us that we should listen well and respond to God's teaching, and Paul warns that mere rhetoric does not make a preacher of the gospel.

Use periods of silence during the service, especially after the readings, for the congregation's response.

Call to Worship

Come to the all-wise Teacher,
   that you may learn
   of the things that last,
   of the truth for your lives.

The Parable of the Sower

Voice 1:   I heard his words. They made sense at the time. That's right, I thought. He's got it in one. But then a friend said 'You don't want to listen to him! He's only a working man – what does he know about the Almighty? Now, if you ask me, the truth is . . .'
And my friend's words made sense, too.

Voice 2:   I heard his words. He certainly convinced me. What he had to say was wonderful news!
I joined his group. I went to his church.
It was great! But then, well, I got this job.
I had to work on Sunday mornings. And the kids don't like me to go out on Sunday night.

Voice 3:   I heard his words. I listened almost to the end – then I remembered I'd left the dinner on too high. And it had started to look like rain and the sheets were still out. And it had occurred to me that I didn't have quite enough wrapping paper for that present – perhaps the newsagent would still be open.
I heard his words – I think.

Voice 4:   I heard his words. And I heard him, too.
           And in him, I found God.

Prayers of Intercession

God of truth, we pray for all seekers after truth,
   for scientists, thinkers, theologians.
L: God of mystery, God of revelation:
R: **Help us in our search for truth**.

God of truth, we pray for all teachers,
   in school or college, university or evening class
   and for those who teach about Christ.
L: God of mystery, God of revelation:
R: **Help us in our search for truth**.

God of truth, we pray for all pupils and students,
   and those in training.
L: God of mystery, God of revelation:
R: **Help us in our search for truth**.

God of truth, we pray for those who provide us with
   information, for writers, journalists and broadcasters.
L: God of mystery, God of revelation:
R: **Help us in our search for truth**.

God of truth, we pray for ourselves
   as we look for lasting truth in a changing world,
   where we often feel lost, confused or betrayed.
L: God of mystery, God of revelation:
R: **Help us in our search for truth**.

In the name of Jesus Christ, your Word, our Truth, the Way.

                                           Amen

Dismissal

Go out into the world as disciples of Christ.
Put all your trust in the Lord.
At every step keep him in mind,
and he will direct your path.

8th Sunday before Easter

Presentation

*The readings for this Sunday give conflicting messages. Job's afflic-
tions are sent to him, with God's permission, as a test of his faith and
not in consequence of any sin. Jesus' miracles are seen as both
healings and acts of making clean, of forgiving sins. So we are
reminded that the subject of healing cannot be tackled in any simplis-
tic way. God is with us in sickness, healing, health and wholeness.
The Job passage could be read by several voices. Ask members of the
congregation to prepare reflections on how illness or disability has
affected their Christian pilgrimage.*

Call to Worship

Let us worship the God
    who showers good gifts upon us.
Let us worship the God
    who longs to make us whole.

Prayer of Confession

Saving God,
we, your people, cry to you
to make us whole.
We are unclean,
diseased by sin,
outcast by selfishness.
We are paralysed
by our inability
to change our own lives.

Saving God, we cry to you
to make us whole,
to cleanse and heal us
that we may stand
and walk with you.
To the leper, the paralysed man, and to us
Jesus, the Son of Man, says,
'Your sins are forgiven.'
Praise to God.   **Amen**

Prayers of Intercession

We pray for a world in need of healing.
　　We bring to God nations afflicted with the diseases
　　of warfare, injustice and poverty. We pray for the
　　wounded soldier, the tortured political prisoner,
　　the child dying of hunger. We remember especially . . .
L:　God who suffers with us:
R:　**Hold us, heal us, save us**.

We pray for a society in need of healing.
　　We bring to God our nation, afflicted with the diseases
　　of materialism, violence and cruelty. We pray for the
　　wealthy but dissatisfied tycoon, the woman afraid to go
　　out alone, the child abused and neglected.
　　We remember especially . . .
L:　God who suffers with us:
R:　**Hold us, heal us, save us**.

We pray for a church in need of healing.
　　We bring to God the church, afflicted with the diseases
　　of disunity, introversion and fear. We pray for the
　　congregation split apart by disagreement, the fellowship
　　group existing only for itself, the church that does
　　not dare to change. We remember especially . . .
L:　God who suffers with us:
R:　**Hold us, heal us, save us**.

We pray for individuals in need of healing.
　　We bring to God humankind, afflicted with diseases
　　of body, mind and spirit. We pray for the woman facing
　　a future of chronic illness, for the schizophrenic and
　　his family, for the believer eaten up with feelings of
　　guilt and worthlessness. We remember especially . . .
L:　God who suffers with us:
R:　**Hold us, heal us, save us**.

We make our prayers in the name of him who came to seek and
save the lost, to heal broken bodies and lives,
Jesus Christ our Lord.　**Amen**

7th Sunday before Easter

Presentation

God is not a remote God, unmoved by our everyday needs. Isaiah promises Israel strength and help from God. Paul miraculously survives a snakebite. And when Jesus accepts the little that is offered him, with God's blessing it becomes abundant food for all. Read Psalm 46 this week.

The Acts reading lends itself to dramatization.

Call to Worship

God is our refuge and our strength,
a very present help in trouble.
The Lord of hosts is with us,
the God of Jacob is our stronghold.

Meditation 'Be still and know that I am God'

Voice 1: I've made it to church just in time.
Overslept again.
I had to get the joint in the oven,
and empty all my handbags to find some cash.

Voice 2: 'Be still and know that I am God.'

Voice 3: I've been at church ages,
here early to see my real friends.
They don't call me names, push and shove me,
like at school. Lord, I get so scared.

Voice 2: 'Be still and know that I am God.'

Voice 4: Of course, it might be nothing,
a small medical problem, easily cured.
It might even go away by itself.
But, God, it could be something more.

Voice 2: 'Be still and know that I am God.'

Voice 5: Lord, I can't find you.
I've looked for you everywhere –
fellowship groups, other churches, big crusades,

I call on you endlessly, but you never reply.

Voice 2: 'Be still and know that I am God.'
Be still, calm your racing thoughts.
Be still, let go of all your fears.
Be still, be quiet, open your hearts to me
in the silence, and know
that I am God.

Silence

Prayer of Offering

Lord, what do I have
that would be a fitting present for you?
You are the Almighty, Creator of the universe,
giver of life, generous beyond thought –
what do I have
that would be a fitting present for you?
Like the five loaves and two fishes
my gifts of money, time and love
seem totally inadequate.
But what I have, I offer to you.
Take my gifts. Bless them.
Use them to feed your hungry world.

Dismissal and Blessing

Do not be afraid to go out
   into a world that does not understand you.
Do not be afraid to love,
   though loving takes and drains and hurts.
Do not be afraid.
For the love of the Creator will protect you,
the resurrection of the Saviour reassure you,
and the power of the Spirit give you strength.
The blessing of the Holy Trinity
   is with us all, now and evermore.   **Amen**

6th Sunday before Easter
Lent 1

Presentation

The theme of temptation lends itself to a variety of visual presentations, perhaps with modern imagery (bear in mind envy is only one of the temptations laid before Jesus). The gospel would be most effectively read by three voices (Jesus, tempter and narrator), and easily dramatized.

Call to Worship *(Rom. 10.9)*

'If on your lips is the confession "Jesus is Lord", and in your hearts the faith that God raised him from the dead, then you will find salvation.'
Let us worship the God of our salvation

Prayer of Confession

Lord God, holy and faithful Father, we come to you as your children. We come to share with you our regret for all of the times when we have forgotten that we are trying to lead the Christian life as followers of Jesus.

There have been times when we have succumbed to the temptations of this life.
– when we have searched out the easy way;
– when we have yearned after worldly things;
– when we have not followed your way;
– when we have tried to live without you.

Help us to remember that people
'cannot live on bread alone'
Help us to remember that we should
'do homage to God and worship him alone'.
Help us to remember not to 'put the Lord to the test'.
May our thoughts, words and deeds
be always guided by these truths.
This prayer we ask through Jesus Christ, our Lord,
who knew what it was to be tempted, but who had the
strength to resist and the courage to overcome. **Amen**

Prayer of Intercession

Lord God, creator and parent, be with those for whom we have special concern this *morning*.

Lord God, we pray for all who have no bread to eat:
– those who hunger and who thirst,
– those who desperately need to know your love.
L: Lord, hear us: R: **Lord, graciously hear us**.

Lord God, we pray for all who have authority over us:
– those who are tempted to abuse their power in politics
   and commerce,
– those who need to find you guiding their lives.
L: Lord, hear us: R: **Lord, graciously hear us**.

Lord God, we pray for all who desire a higher status:
– those who in seeking more for themselves give less to
   others,
– those who always look to others to help them, without
   trying to help themselves,
– those who only believe because of what they think they
   can get from you.
L: Lord, hear us: R: **Lord, graciously hear us**.

Lord God, we pray for people from our own church family:
– those who are unwell, anxious or in any kind of need,
– those who need you to feed them with the Bread of Life,
– those who need you to comfort and support them,
– those who need to be lifted up by you,
   especially we pray for . . . may they know your love for them.
L: Lord, hear us: R: **Lord, graciously hear us**.

Lord God, we thank you for giving us the strength
– to resist temptation in our lives;
– to forget our own needs and help others;
– to serve rather than expecting to be served;
– to resist the temptation to wield power.
May we learn from the example of all who live alongside the people in greatest need, and from your Son.   **Amen**

5th Sunday before Easter
Lent 2

Presentation

The readings for today are a little 'strong' for all-age worship, but are an important part of our heritage. We cannot avoid them but they need careful use and perhaps some retelling or explanation. With a story or role play show how even 'good' people can do wrong, or how a family can be split apart by selfishness or lies.

Prayer of Confession

'The Lord God saw the whole world was corrupt
and full of violence.'
Lord, we are sorry
    that human beings have spoilt the world you gave to
    them, spoilt it with greed, selfishness and violence.
We are sorry
    that we only seem able to settle our differences
    through war, that our desire for more wealth leads to
    theft, that we abuse the love and trust you gave us.

Jesus said 'He who is not with me is against me':
Lord, we are sorry
    that we have spoilt the life you have given to us;
    spoilt it through ignorance, complacency and blindness
    to the truth.
We are sorry
    that even when we try to live better lives, we fail you
    and go against your ways.
We are sorry
    for the times when we have caused hurt to people
    unknowingly.
We are sorry that we do not live perfect lives.

Lord, drive out the evil within us,
forgive us all our sins and fill us with your love.   **Amen**

Offering Prayer

Accept our gifts of money and help us to use them wisely in the
work of the church, according to your will.   **Amen**

Prayer of Intercession

God, our heavenly Father we hold before you in our prayers all whose faith is tested today:

– Those who live openly by faith, even in countries
   where few people feel part of your family.
Help us to follow their example.

– Those who put their faith into practice, even in
   difficult or dangerous circumstances.
Help us to follow their example.

– Those who speak about their faith, even when oppressed
   for their beliefs.
Help us to follow their example.

Help us, and all who have become weak in faith, to know you, understand you and be your faithful witnesses.   **Amen**

Prayer of Dedication

Lord God, we offer our lives to you.
We came as your family to worship and adore you, we leave as your family dedicated to serve you in the world.
Wherever we go, whoever we meet, in whatever circumstances we find ourselves, we pray that we may be worthy to bear the name of your Son, Jesus Christ, in whose name we offer our prayers.   **Amen**

Blessing

As the Lord saved Noah and his family on the Ark,
   may God carry you safely through the floods of life.
As Jesus saved the world by his death on the cross,
   may he keep you safe from temptation.
As the Spirit of God saves people from error,
   may God guide you in all truth.
And the blessing of God, Father, Son and Holy Spirit,
   go with you today, and for ever.   **Amen**

4th Sunday before Easter
Lent 3

Presentation

The gospel could be read in parts or dramatized. In Verses 23–27 use the congregation as 'everybody'. With some preparation there is scope for mime or liturgical dance.

Call to Worship

Who do we come to worship?
Is it John the Baptist? **No!** Is it Elijah? **No!**
Is it one of the prophets? **No!** Is it God's Messiah? **Yes!**
Then sing out in praise of the Son of Man.

Prayer of Confession

We say that we are your followers, but don't follow your
  example.
We say that we love you, but love ourselves more.
We say that we are prepared to carry a cross for you, but put it
  down as soon as we can.
We say that we want to save our lives, but put ourselves in
  danger of losing them.
Lord, help us pick up the cross of obedience and to carry the
cross of sacrifice. Lift off our load of sin and guilt and give us the
strength to be your servants. May you never have reason to be
ashamed of us. Forgive us all our faults and let us see the
Kingdom of God. **Amen**

Prayer of Intercession

We offer our prayers for all humankind, and especially for those
who reveal the glory of Christ in the world.
For people who proclaim your holy word:
– ministers and preachers, especially . . . ;
– chaplains to industry, prisons, hospitals, the armed
  forces and centres of education, especially . . . ;
L: You are the Christ: R: **We glorify your name.**

For all who take your holy word into the world:
- those who in schools, on street corners, through television and radio, tell the good news to people who have never heard it before;
- evangelists and missionaries at home and abroad;
- those from other races and cultures who enrich our knowledge of God;
- those who, as our brothers and sisters in Christ share their faith, especially . . . ;

L: You are the Christ: R: **We glorify your name**.

For those who share and teach us your holy word:
- those who, on Sundays and throughout the week work with children and young people;
- those who first inspired faith in us
- and those who encourage and support us now;
- for leaders of *fellowship groups*, especially . . . ;

L: You are the Christ: R: **We glorify your name**.

For those who are forbidden to speak your holy word:
- those who are persecuted and suffer because they proclaim you as their Lord;
- those who are imprisoned for their faith;
- those who challenge the lack of justice and equality in the countries where they live, especially . . . ;

L: You are the Christ: R: **We glorify your name**.

For all who find it hard to express your holy word:
- those who have doubts,
- those who are weighed down by illness or worry,
- and those who have lost the faith they once had, especially . . . ;
- for each one of us, as we try to declare your name in a world which cannot be bothered to listen.

L: You are the Christ: R: **We glorify your name.   Amen**

Dismissal   *Ask the congregation to focus on a cross*

The cross – Christ has died on it.
The cross – we will look to it.
The cross – we are saved by it.
The cross – we will carry it.
Go with the cross of Christ before you.

Ex. 34.29–35
II Cor. 3.4–18
Luke 9.28–36

3rd Sunday before Easter

Lent 4 (Also see Mothering Sunday)

Presentation

A mirror reflecting the sun or a bright light (torch) could begin to explain how we reveal God's glory. A smiling or sad face reflects our feelings – how do we reflect God in our lives? Cover the face with a cloth to show how we veil (hide) God from others.

Point out how the Luke reading follows on from last week's lection when the disciples recognize Jesus as the Messiah.

Call to Worship

The glory of God shines in the world.
　It shines in the beauty of creation.
　It shines in the good news about Jesus.
　It shines in the love we find in others.
Let us reflect the glory of God in our praise and worship.

Prayer of Confession　　*Could be used responsively*

The wonders of creation reflect the glory of God:
Lord, forgive us when we spoil them.
Human beings reflect the glory of God:
Lord, forgive us when we abuse one another.
The Commandments reflect the glory of God:
Lord, forgive us when we break them.
The love of Jesus reflects the glory of God:
Lord, forgive us when we forget it.
The power of the Spirit reflects the glory of God:
Lord, forgive us when we ignore you.

Lord, forgive us whenever we turn our faces from you and do not reflect the love you show to us each day.
Transform us into your likeness and set us free to serve wherever your Spirit leads us.　**Amen**

Prayer of Offering

Lord, all the riches we have come from you,
　wealth, happiness, comfort, faith, love.
As we offer our gifts of money, accept our lives, and guide and help us to use them wisely and well.　**Amen**

Prayer of Thanksgiving

Lord God we thank you for all your goodness to us.

We thank you for the faithfulness of Moses:
– for his teaching and his commitment to your way,
– for his obedience to your will,
– and for the glow of your presence which shone through
him.

We thank you for the faithfulness of Jesus:
– for his preaching and healing,
– for his obedience even to his death on a cross,
– and for your transfiguring glory which shone through
him.

We thank you for the faithfulness of your servants through the
ages:
– for their sharing of faith and hope,
– for their obedience in the tasks to which you called
them
– and for the divine love which shone through them.

We thank you for the faithfulness of all who serve you today:
– for their pastoral care and evangelism,
– for their obedience in going wherever you send them,
– and for the example of loving service which shines
through them.

We thank you for the faithfulness you inspire in us:
– may we be true witnesses to your good news,
– may we be obedient to you in all we say and do
– and may we reflect your love which shines on our lives.

Amen

Blessing

The Lord bless you with joy.
The Lord bless you with peace.
The Lord bless you with love.
You chosen ones of God,
give glory to the Father, Son and Holy Spirit.

YEAR C
Mothering Sunday
(Also see 3rd Sunday before Easter)

Gen. 21.8–21
Gal. 4.21–5.1
Luke 1.39–45

Presentation

Mothering Sunday has many roots and traditions and is usually marked as a happy day in church life. The readings tell of both the joys and the problems of being a mother. It is important, however, to remember that not every woman in the congregation will be a mother and that those who are do not always find motherhood a joy. Sensitive handling of the readings (especially Gal. 4.27) and prayers is necessary. Some churches recognize this day as Cradle Roll (First Steps) Sunday and present a gift of flowers or a card to the mothers at the service – be careful to include all the women present.
  Ask women to read the lessons, lead the prayers, etc.

Call to Worship

This place is our spiritual home;
  here we meet God, here we learn how to live,
  here we find comfort, support and security.
Let us praise God through Jesus, son of Mary.

Prayer of Thanksgiving

Loving God, you created us female and male and gave us the opportunity to love and create other human beings.
We thank you for our mothers and those who have shown us what motherhood can be:
– caring for their children from the moment of birth;
– maintaining love and concern as they grow and develop;
– showing a continued interest into adult life.

Loving God, you chose women to bear sons and daughters for your work, giving us all a fine example to follow.
We thank you for the example of mothers in the Bible:
– for the anguished concern of Hagar;
– the patience of Sarah;
– the foresight of Elizabeth;
– and the devotion of Mary.

52

Loving God, because we know you as our parent, and experience
the depth of your love,
we thank you especially for the inspiring example of mothers
whose concern extends beyond their family circle:
- offering to foster or adopt children in need;
- working with broken families in their community;
- supporting charitable causes.
Loving God, we thank you for all mothers and the ways in which
you mother us.   **Amen**

Intercessions for parents and children

Children are:
   small lives but big responsibilities;
   small bodies but big demands.
Let us pray for all homes, that they may be
- places of love and support;
- places of acceptance and security;
- places of forgiveness and tolerance;
- places where both adults and children can grow and
  develop and be themselves.
Let us pray for all parents:
- that they may create loving, caring homes;
- that they may treat their children as persons;
- that they may accept that there is no such thing as
  a perfect parent or perfect child;
- that they may not be overwhelmed with guilt;
- that they may have joy in their children.
Let us pray for all children:
- that they may have a happy and secure childhood;
- that they may not be warped or spoilt in any way;
- that they may learn to cope with themselves and
  with others;
- that they may grow up to be loving, caring adults.
Help us, Lord, to work together, and with you, in home, church
and community to make the society we have prayed for into a
living reality.
May all children feel part of your rule of love,
in the name of your son, Jesus Christ.   **Amen**

2nd Sunday before Easter
Lent 5   Passion Sunday

Presentation

The gospel reading helps us to understand why the Scribes and Pharisees opposed Jesus and begins to set the scene for his arrest and trial. It is better dramatized (mimed) or read in parts than used as a reading for one voice.

The Hebrews lesson could precede the intercessions.

Call to Worship

'The stone which the builders rejected
turned out to be the most important of all.'
Let us worship God through his Son Jesus Christ,
the keystone of our lives and focus of our praise.

Prayer of Confession

Lord of the world, as we confess our faults,
hear us and forgive:
– we are sorry that we violate both the land and sea,
   plundering their resources without a care,
   and exploiting our brothers and sisters.   *Silence*
Forgive us.

– we are sorry that we carry anger and hatred in our
   hearts, treating others shamefully
   and causing trouble and strife.   *Silence*
Forgive us.

– we are sorry that we are selfish and proud,
   shutting ourselves off from our neighbours,
   and closing our minds to their needs.   *Silence*
Forgive us.

Forgive us that we abuse your creation,
fail to reflect your love and ignore your will.
Help us to mend our ways.

We thank you for the coming of Jesus into the world
and for the new life he brings. We praise you that, through his

death and resurrection, we receive forgiveness and are set once
more on the right path.
Lord of the world, help us to use all that we receive from your
generous love gratefully, wisely and as Jesus has taught
us.   **Amen**

Prayer of Intercession

Almighty Father, as we pray for this troubled world,
help us to discern your presence in it.

We see war and conflict,
   hatred between ethnic groups, racial discrimination,
   and are tempted to lose heart.
   But you never despair of humankind.
L: Lord, give peace to the world:
R: **And increase our faith**.

We see sickness and suffering,
   anxiety and loneliness, fear and mourning,
   and the pain overwhelms us.
   But you share that pain and never draw back.
L: Lord, give comfort to the world:
R: **And increase our faith**.

We see empty churches,
   people without a purpose, new gods taking your place,
   and our courage fails us.
   But your love is never deterred or outfaced.
L: Lord, give hope to the world:
R: **And increase our faith**.

Lord, give us eyes to see your work around us and in our hearts,
and use our prayers to transform the world by your everlasting
love.   **Amen**

A Dismissal Thought

Do not trip over the stone and fall from grace,
but stand on the rock of salvation and rise to glory.

Sunday before Easter
Lent 6   Palm Sunday

Presentation

Plan a dramatic enactment of the entry into Jerusalem as local conditions allow; a parade round the Junior Church rooms would add to the excitement, using the door to the church as the entry into the city. Wave palms and lay coats across the path of Jesus and the disciples. As some walk, others could sing a lively hymn or chorus focussing on 'Hosanna'. It may be that only the Luke reading is considered suitable for all ages; continue to verse 40 for the note of celebration which contrasts with the sombre mood of the coming Holy Week.

Call to Worship

Use Psalm 24.7–10, with shouts and acclamations coming from different parts of the building; balcony, choir stalls, etc. around the congregation.

Prayer of Adoration and Intercession

Lord God, we greet you on this day of celebration.
L: Hosanna!   R: **Hosanna to the Son of David!**
We praise you for the faithful obedience of the disciples.
L: Hosanna!   R: **Hosanna to the Son of David!**
We praise you for those who shouted with expectation.
L: Hosanna!   R: **Hosanna to the Son of David!**
We pray for those who proclaim you today.
L: Hosanna!   R: **Hosanna to the Son of David!**
We pray for all who hear your message of love.
L: Hosanna!   R: **Hosanna to the Son of David!**
We pray for those who still do not know you.
L: Hosanna!   R: **Hosanna to the Son of David!**

Amen

Prayer of Thanksgiving and Dedication

Lord God, on this day of celebration
– we come to thank you for the coming of Jesus:
– we remember his entry into Jerusalem,

and we thank you for his courage;
- we recall the events of the week ahead,
  and we thank you for his dedication;
- we reflect on the agony of Good Friday,
  and we thank you for his forgiving love;
- we are reminded of the crowds shouting 'Hosanna',
  and we thank you for all who have praised him
  over the years and who help us worship today.

Lord God, on this day of celebration
  we dedicate ourselves in your service:
  like the people of Jerusalem,
  we greet you, we shout your praise;
  but not with cloaks and palm branches alone,
  for we offer all that we have and are,
  all that we will have and may yet become,
  in thanks for all that we have received from you.
We bring ourselves to you. Bless us in your service.
Lord God, on this day of dedication, we thank you for Jesus.

Amen

Meditation   *Based on Luke 19.40. Use two voices*

Listen, listen, can you not hear the shouts of praise?
     'Hosanna in the highest.
   Blessed is he who comes in the name of the Lord!'
Keep quiet, keep quiet, restrain your disciples Master.
     'Hosanna in the highest.
   Blessed is he who comes in the name of the Lord!'
Listen, listen, even the stones shout with praise.
     'Hosanna in the highest.
   Blessed is he who comes in the name of the Lord!'

Dismissal

Go with us, heavenly Father, in the power of your Spirit.
Strengthen and encourage us
in all that we do to worship and serve you.
Guide us through the coming week, and never let our shouts of
praise waver in the face of suffering or despair.
We ask it in the name of Jesus Christ our Lord.   **Amen**

Easter Day

Presentation

An Easter garden could provide a focus, perhaps under the communion table. Make sure the tomb is open.

The Luke reading keeps the continuity with Palm Sunday. Luke's account includes a number of characters – allocate 'parts' to individual readers or use drama.

Call to Worship

Alleluia! Christ is risen!
Alleluia! Christ is risen!   *Repeat once or twice*
The tomb is open, Jesus is alive!
Alleluia! Christ is risen!
We come to worship with songs of gladness and praise!
Alleluia! Christ is risen!

Introduction to prayers   *Based on the Luke account*

Try to imagine how it was on that first Easter morning . . . the disciples feeling utterly desolate . . . all their hopes ended in the sad and awful scenes of three days before . . . Mary and the other women standing in the garden in the cool morning air . . . afraid, not knowing what to expect . . . the followers of Jesus in confusion and fearing for their own lives . . .
    The news breaks – and what news it is!
Tell the Easter Story

Prayer of Praise

God, break into our humdrum lives with your astounding good news, and fill us with joy and hope.
All too often we are apprehensive and afraid of what life has in store for us,
    we lack confidence in ourselves and in you,
    we let you down by not trusting your words.
Even today we are like the women gathering at the tomb, uncertain of what to expect.
Help us to understand the message of Easter, so that it can transform our lives and raise us to new life.

Show us the significance of the empty tomb, the meaning of the
words of promise 'on the third day he will rise',
and give us the grace to believe.
The Lord is Risen: R: **He is risen indeed! Alleluia!**

Lord God, we adore you, we praise you, we exalt you.
   we worship you through the risen, living Christ.
As we raise our voices in song and lift our hearts in prayer, fill us
with the hope of resurrection.   **Amen**

Prayer of Thanksgiving

Father, we thank you for raising Jesus from the dead and opening
the way to heaven for all.
We thank you for the glory of that first Easter morning,
   for the signs of new life in the world,
   for the glorious Easter message of hope.
Help us to proclaim these marvellous things, confident of even
more marvellous things to come.
In the name of the risen Jesus.   **Amen**

Response for the prayers of intercession

L: The Lord hears our prayer: R: **Alleluia! Alleluia!**

Prayer of Commitment

The stone was rolled away from the tomb and the disciples saw
that Jesus had risen, freed from death to new life.
Risen Lord,
free us from all that holds us back from serving you,
   from all that keeps us from loving you,
   from all that stops us seeking your kingdom,
   from all that hardens us from helping others,
   from sharing your risen life.   **Amen**

Dismissal

Go in hope, the risen Lord goes before you.
Go in peace, the risen Lord goes with you.
Go in love, the risen Lord lives within you.

1st Sunday after Easter

Presentation

It is still 'good news' that Jesus is risen. All three readings are about sharing good news. The passage from II Kings needs an explanatory introduction and, although not normally associated with Easter, could shed new light on it. It includes elements similar to those found in the Emmaus Road story: despair, doubt, recognition, prophecy and good news. The 'Emmaus Road' is well known and could be dramatized. Worship, especially if Holy Communion is included, could be constructed around the unfolding of the story.

Call to Worship (*Rev. 19.6–7*)

Hallelujah! The Lord our God, sovereign over all, has entered on his reign! Let us rejoice and shout for joy,
and pay homage to him.

Prayer of Praise

How your Son, the risen Christ,
lifted the hearts of the travellers on the Emmaus Road!
When we need you most you come and walk with us still, giving us:
– hope in our despair;
– friendship in our loneliness;
– strength in our struggling;
– light in our darkness;
– comfort in our sorrow.

Help us always to discern your presence, to respond in thanks and praise, and to rejoice that nothing can separate us from your love in Christ Jesus, our risen Lord.   **Amen**

Prayer before the Scriptures or Sermon

Lord, break the Bread of Life for us today,
making plain to us the meaning of your Word.
And grant us wisdom to discern the truth,

dedication to put it into practice
and hope to face all that the future may bring.
May our hearts be on fire with the gospel of Christ.   **Amen**

Prayers of Intercession

God of every time and place,
we pray for those who are in difficulty on life's journey:
 – those who are searching for you and need to be assured
   that their quest can be successful;
 – those who are seeking meaning for their lives and need
   understanding of your Word;
 – those who are making genuine discoveries but need
   guidance as they learn;
 – those who walk in darkness and despair and need the
   light and comfort of Christ.
We pray for those who walk alongside these travellers,
   helping them on their journey
   and sharing with them the insights of faith.

Open our eyes, Lord, to recognize Jesus
   walking with us on our journey through life.
Open our minds, Lord, to understand the good news
   of resurrection and hope for the future.
Open our hearts, Lord, to receive the broken bread
   of love you offer to us.
Through the risen Christ.   **Amen**

Words of Dismissal (*II Kings 7.9b adapted*)

This is a day of good news, do not keep it to yourselves.
Go now and give the good news to the King's people.

May the risen Jesus walk with you, talk with you,
stay with you and inspire you,
and may you live for ever in God's presence
and share this good news with others.   **Amen**

YEAR C

2nd Sunday after Easter

Presentation

How do you know that something, or someone, is alive? You might look at them, touch them, listen to them. Using a stone, a seed, a plant, an animal and a person, examine how you detect life. Luke is stressing that Jesus has risen from death in human form, and Isaiah contrasts things dead and alive (Isa. 51.3).

Call to Worship *(Isa. 51.4)*

These are the words of the Lord:
  'Pay heed to me, my people, and listen to me, my nation,
  for instruction will shine forth from me and my
  judgment will be a light to peoples.'

Prayer of Adoration

It is too wonderful to believe,
  it is incredible, astounding,
  too good to be true
  – that Jesus has risen from the dead
  and appeared to the disciples.

It is too much to grasp,
  it is challenging, comforting,
  can it be true
  – that Jesus sits at God's right hand
  and has all authority over heaven and earth?

It is too amazing for words,
  it is exciting, exhilarating,
  it is true
  – that Jesus continues to be with us
  and pours out his Father's love upon us!

Sometimes the truth is so important that it overwhelms us.
We praise you, great God, for making these things happen,
and trust you to continue your work in our lives. **Amen**

Prayer of Intercession

It seems so final:
- the world is continually torn apart by wars,
- the environment is ruined by our greed,
- love is extinguished by hatred,
- joy is overshadowed by sorrow.

L: Lord of resurrection: R: **Show your saving power**.

It seems so final:
- friendships are destroyed by angry words,
- families are separated through lack of love,
- future plans are shattered by illness,
- relationships are broken by death.

L: Lord of resurrection: R: **Show your saving power**.

It seems so final:
- the crucifixion of a Saviour,
- the disappearance of a Master,
- the loss of a Friend and Guide,
- the lack of a Shepherd for the sheep.

L: Lord of resurrection: R: **Show your saving power**.

Teach us, Lord,
that with you nothing is final except your loving purpose.
Yours will be the last word, the final act,
the decision that the end has come.
Until then, may we entrust ourselves to your care, and may the
power of the resurrection transform our lives and your world. In
the name of the risen Christ.   **Amen**

Words of Dismissal (*I Cor. 15.58*)

My friends, stand firm and immovable, and work for the Lord
always, work without limit, since you know that in the Lord your
labour cannot be lost.

May the risen Jesus be with you, go with you,
strengthen you and fill you with hope,
so that you may live forever in the Lord's presence
and work to his glory.   **Amen**

3rd Sunday after Easter

Presentation

In some resurrection stories Jesus eats bread as if to prove he has really risen. This week the readings are about bread for life (manna in the wilderness) and the Bread of Life (eternal life through Jesus).
    Talk about what we need to live – bread and faith.

Opening Words (*John 6.40*)

Jesus said, 'It is my Father's will that everyone who sees
the Son and has faith in him should have eternal life;
and I will raise them up on the last day.'

Prayer of Confession

Forgive us, Lord, when we are not satisfied with our lot in life:
– always wanting something more, something different;
– thinking that we know better than you;
– priding ourselves on our achievements;
– concentrating on the things of this world, rather than
    the values of your kingdom.
Forgive us Lord,
– our greed,
– our presumption,
– our smugness,
– and our false values.
Lift us from complaining to praising,
    from sin to righteousness,
    from death to life,
through the saving power of the risen Christ.   **Amen**

Offering Prayer

Giver of manna in the wilderness,
giver of bread in communion,
giver of life eternal,

One and only God, from whom are all things and for whom we exist, with thanks we offer our gifts.   **Amen**

Prayers of Intercession

White bread, brown bread, sliced bread, granary bread:
Lord, we have a choice of bread to eat.
We pray for those without enough food to live,
deprived of bread because of drought, famine or greed.
L: Bread of Life: R: **Feed the world**.

Civil war, terrorism, nuclear threat, armed conflict:
Lord, we continually fight to gain our own way.
We pray for those caught up in hatred,
deprived of peace because of misused political power.
L: Bread of Life: R: **Feed the world**.

Doubt, despair, bereavement, hopelessness:
Lord, we need your presence with us at all times.
We pray for those overwhelmed by anxiety, and deprived of hope
because they do not know or trust you.
L: Bread of Life: R: **Feed the world**.

Arrogance, pride, complacency, lack of faith:
Lord, we seek your Spirit to transform our lives.
We pray for ourselves, deprived of the assurance of eternal life
because we are not open to your love.
L: Bread of Life: R: **Feed the world**.

Lord, we come to you in our need:
   hungering for hope,
   thirsting to know you better,
   and seeking your way.
Enrich our lives with all that is good
and so fill us with the glory of heaven,
that we may praise your name forever.   **Amen**

Blessing

May God feed and sustain you on life's journey.
May God encourage and strengthen you in your discipleship.
May God bless you, with the gifts and fruits of the Holy Spirit.
Now and forever more.   **Amen**

4th Sunday after Easter

Presentation

One theme which connects the three readings is our relationship with God. God loved the people of Israel (Deut. 7.8), Jesus is our friend (John 15.14), we are all one in Christ and heirs to God's promise (Gal. 3.28 and 4.7). Paul, in calling Christians 'sons', is saying they (and, by implication, we) can have the same relationship with the Father as Jesus. Talk about the rights, privileges, duties and responsibilities of being in a relationship (family or friendship) and how we must live as members of God's family – 'Love one another, as I have loved you.'

Call to Worship

God first chose us, cared for us, loved us. As the children of God we are privileged to call him 'Abba, Father!'
Sons and daughters of God, let us worship God,
by whom we are all one, in union with Christ Jesus.

Prayer of Praise

Father God,
　　you created the world and set us in it:
　　you cared for your people and loved them;
　　you gave an oath to Abraham and promised to bless all
　　his descendants;
　　you made a covenant with Moses and the people of Israel.
L: You are our God and we are your people:
R: **We love you, Lord**.

Father God,
　　you sent your Son into the world:
　　through him you spoke to us of love,
　　your love for us and our love for others.
　　He revealed your love by his death and resurrection,
　　and he called us his friends.
L: You are our God and we are your people:
R: **We love you, Lord**.

Father God,
  you poured out your Holy Spirit on the world:
  you set us free from the chains of sin;
  you raise us from death to new life;
  you live in the hearts of all who love you;
  you invite us to call you 'Abba' and give us your
  inheritance of eternal life.
L: You are our God and we are your people:
R: **We love you, Lord**.

Father God,
  we, your loving children, praise you:
  filled by your Spirit, we praise you;
  united in Christ Jesus, we praise you.
L: You are our God and we are your people:
R: **We love you, Lord.**   **Amen**

Prayer of Confession   *Use different voices*

Forgive us, Lord,
when we don't see beyond the labels that we put on people.
  'I am *white* and you are *black*.'
  'I am a *worker* and you are a *boss*.'
  'I am *female* and you are *male*.'
  'I am *saved* and you are *damned*.'

Forgive us for making judgments which distinguish between
    those who are like us and those who are not,
    those whom we like and those whom we choose not to like,
    those whom we love and those whom we don't.
Teach us that through Jesus, master and friend of us all, we are
set free to love one another.
May we know his forgiveness, and be able to love others,
regardless of age, sex, class, race, as he loves us. In Christ
nothing divides us if we follow his commands. Thank you God,
for your love and mercy.   **Amen**

Dismissal (*John 15.16, 11*)

God's chosen, go on and bear fruit, fruit that will last,
so that Jesus' joy may be in you and your joy complete.

5th Sunday after Easter

Presentation

The readings today are about faith – keeping faith, having faith and staying faithful. The examples of faith are more important than the miracles associated with them. Modern parallels from the world church would help explain the point – keeping faith under persecution, having faith when humble, staying faithful despite outside pressures.

Both Daniel and Luke could be dramatized or at least read in parts.

Opening Words (*II Thess. 3.5*)

May the Lord direct your hearts towards God's love
and the steadfastness of Christ.

Prayer of Adoration

We praise you, ever faithful God,
for always guiding, healing and caring for your people.

Through exile and persecution
you never failed the people of Israel
and, when they were disobedient, you never turned away.

You sent your Son, born as one of us,
and, even when he was rejected and nailed to the cross,
your love was never deterred or defeated.

You sent your Spirit, bringer of hope and comfort,
who continually inspires the worship and service
of all who love you.

Your love is everlasting:
mighty as mountains, refreshing as streams,
warming our hearts as the sun warms our bodies.

In faith we worship and adore you,
ever living, ever loving, ever faithful God.   **Amen**

Prayer of Confession   *Linked to the three readings.*
We want to be like Daniel,
   faithful in prayer and worship,
   regardless of pressure to conform to the will of others.
L: Forgive our lack of faith:
R: **And have mercy on us**.

We want to be like the centurion,
   trusting in Jesus to respond to our prayer,
   regardless of other people's scepticism.
L: Forgive our lack of faith:
R: **And have mercy on us**.

We want to be like Paul,
   believing in the Lord and having confidence in him,
   regardless of wrong-headed or wicked people without
   faith.
L: Forgive our lack of faith:
R: **And have mercy on us**.

Lord, help us to trust and obey you, and fill our hearts with your
love, that we may be witnesses to your glory.   **Amen**

Prayer of Petition

Almighty God, forgive us that, when we pray,
we expect you to do as we say.
Give us humility in prayer, acknowledging that
we are not worthy to ask anything of you.
And when our prayers seem not to be answered,
at least in the way we want,
help us to trust your wisdom and accept your will.
Keep us faithful to you, never doubting your power,
and ready to be your servants in all things.   **Amen**

Words of Dismissal (*II Thess. 3.3*)
The Lord is faithful, he will strengthen you
and guard you from the evil one. **Thanks be to God**.

6th Sunday after Easter
Sunday after Ascension Day

Presentation

After the Ascension the disciples begin to pick up the pieces. A discussion about beginning again – after a weekend, a holiday, a change in school or career, a house removal or similar upheaval – would help the congregation to think what it meant for Jesus to leave the disciples. Things will never be the same but life has to continue; and what has gone before is not lost, but the basis for a new start. Ezekiel can be extended to verse 14 (try mime). In Acts 1 (read in parts) you may choose to omit verses 19 and 20.

Opening Words   (*Ezek. 37.14*)

'Then I shall put my spirit into you and you will come to life . . . and you shall know that I the Lord have spoken.'

Prayer of Adoration

We adore you, God,
    for you created the earth.
    Everything we see, smell, touch, taste and hear,
    was made by you in your goodness.

We adore you, God,
    for you are 'down to earth'.
    You sent your Son into the world,
    to live as we live, and die as we die.

We adore you, God,
    for you are above the earth.
    You are beyond time and space, a marvellous mystery,
    and there is always more to know about you.

We adore you, God,
    for in the incarnation and the ascension,
    you bridged the gap between things human and divine.
    You understand things temporal and, in Jesus,
    you opened for us the way to things eternal.

God of heaven and earth, we adore you.   **Amen**

Meditation

'What is going to happen now?'
How the disciples must have wondered why their friend Jesus
wanted them to gather at the mountain top.
Some knelt in worship – here was the Lord!
Others were doubtful – unsure even now.
What had they witnessed?
A life of love? A death of forgiveness?
The resurrection of a man? The salvation of God?
As Jesus came near to them
they saw a new radiance, he was confident and smiling.
It was if he knew he had achieved his task,
and now he was to receive some reward.
'Full authority has been committed to me.'
This man was in control,
in charge of himself and in charge of the world.
'Go therefore to all nations and make them my disciples.'
They knew what to do – baptize in the name of God;
and what to say – teach these commandments.
But could they manage to do it?
Yes, because they were not to be alone.
They had seen the Son and in him they had seen the Father.
But he was not leaving them, he gave them that promise.
'I will be with you always, to the end of time.'
To look at him, and to see his glory, was to believe
that anything and everything was possible.

Prayer for Guidance   *Praying for the future*

You know the hearts of everyone, Lord.
We seek your guidance for this church and our lives.
You know our faith, our gifts and our needs.
In silence we listen for your word to us.   *Silence*
May we do your will.   **Amen**

Words of Dismissal

Bear witness for Jesus wherever you go,
and the blessing of God shall be with you.

Pentecost

Presentation

*God communicates through – and in spite of – our differing cultures.
The coming of God's Holy Spirit has the same meaning, in whatever
language you hear it. The readings from Genesis and Acts both
mention speaking in different languages. A greeting could be given in
several languages at the start of worship, or a 'universal' language
like Latin – perhaps a Taizé chant – used at some point. The Luke
reading would lend itself to drama: bring out the point that we should
always have the confidence to ask for what we need, both materially
and spiritually. A feeling of celebration can be stimulated by the use
of symbolic colours, the congregation being encouraged to wear
clothes, buttonholes and ribbons, in the red and white of Pentecost.*

Call to Worship

Different though we are, we are God's people
and we come together to worship, united in Jesus.
He will surely give the Holy Spirit to those who ask him!

Opening Prayer

Father, we praise you: your love for us is constantly renewed and
your generosity never fails.
You came to us in Jesus,
and your Holy Spirit is always with us.
We thank you that we have heard this good news
in our own language and understood it.
We thank you that, with your help, we have welcomed your
Spirit, drawn closer to you and begun to lead new lives.
We pray that, gladly accepting all your good gifts,
we may use them to help others and to make plain your gracious
goodness.
May we rejoice to be your people and to reflect the light and love
of Christ and the power of the Holy Spirit.
We ask it in Jesus's name.   **Amen**

Prayer of Petition

Dear God, our loving Father,
We ask   that you will pour out your Holy Spirit on your
          church, so that as we receive its power, we may grow
          to be more like Jesus.
We seek   to know your will for us, and to find how we may
          serve in love.
We knock on the door knowing that you will open it and let us
          into your eternal life.
We pray   together in the words which Jesus taught his friends:
          Our Father . . .

Prayer of Dedication

Holy Spirit of God,
    Spirit of truth, freedom and unity,
    You have freed us from the curse of Babel,
    uniting us, and giving us understanding.
Today we become one in you,
    all brothers and sisters,
    no one alone, and no one isolated.
Today you give us life and inspiration
    and call us to share them with others.
Today you give us freedom, justice and peace,
    and call us to liberate all who are in bondage,
    to work for justice and to become peace-makers.
We pray for one another,
asking that you will remain with us and in us,
now and forever.   **Amen**

Final words

Fire our hearts with the warmth of your love,
    fan the flames of enthusiasm to serve you,
        let us burn with joy from being at one with you!

Followed by sharing the grace

1st Sunday after Pentecost
Trinity Sunday

Presentation

St Patrick used a shamrock leaf (like a clover) to help people understand the Trinity: a clover leaf each, to take home afterwards, will be a useful visual aid. Use the Te Deum (selected parts) as an introduction to worship.

Call to Worship

Marvelling at the mystery and wonder of the universe to which we belong:
Let us worship God the Creator.
Remembering Jesus and his ministry which revealed the Father's glory:
Let us worship God the Saviour.
Acknowledging the presence of love around and within us;
Let us worship God the Holy Spirit.

Prayer of Approach

Eternal God, far beyond all we can imagine and yet present with us as we pray, we praise you for showing yourself as Father, Son and Holy Spirit, three in one and one in three.

God our Father;
– you are eternal,
– parent of all creation;
– you created us in your image,
– you love us and forgive us at all times,
– you inspire our praise and worship in all places,
– you care for us, and on that we depend.
L: Father God: R: **We worship and adore you.**

God the Son, Jesus Christ;
– you came in Palestine in human form,
– and you continually come to us where we are,
– you died for us on the cross,
– and you meet us in our neighbours;

– you opened new life for us by your resurrection,
– you feed us with the bread of life.
L: Jesus Christ, Son of God: R: **We worship and adore you**.

God the Holy Spirit;
– you are the life and love of God in everyone,
– you prompt our wonder,
– you fill us with joy,
– you bring order to our chaotic lives,
– you fire us with your freedom,
– you fill us with your power.
L: Holy Spirit of God: R: **We worship and adore you**.

Eternal God, one in three and three in one, we worship and
adore you. All glory and praise to you, now and always.   **Amen**

Prayer of Confession

When we lose faith in the goodness of creation,
and in your father-like love,
L: Lord God: R: **Forgive us**.

When we lose faith in Jesus as the true reflection of all that you
are,
L: Lord God: R: **Forgive us**.

When we lose faith in the Holy Spirit's presence with us, helping,
strengthening, enabling, guiding,
L: Lord God: R: **Forgive us**.

In God we're bound, all around, by the Trinity.
We give thanks to the Father, the Son and the Holy
Spirit.   **Amen**

Final Words

We give our lips, our hearts, our minds, our strength,
to serve you, O God, and to love our neighbours,
in the name of Jesus and in the power of the Holy Spirit.   **Amen**

II Sam. 7.4–16
Acts 2.37–47
Luke 14.15–24

2nd Sunday after Pentecost

Presentation

'Surprise' is a theme found in this week's readings. God is not tied to any time or place and cannot be contained. Despite our best efforts to put God 'in a box', he continually breaks out to surprise us. Those whom he invites to be part of the Kingdom may also be a surprise to us. Perhaps some surprise element could be included in the worship and used as a teaching point (Jack-in-a-box).

The Luke reading could be dramatized, perhaps in a modern interpretation or as a mime.

Find a suitable song which echoes this theme.

Call to Worship (*from Psalm 95*)

Come! Let us raise a joyful song to the Lord,
a shout of triumph to the rock of our salvation.
Enter in! Let us bow down in worship,
let us kneel before the Lord, who made us,
for he is our God, we are the people he shepherds, the flock in his care.

Prayer of Praise

Living Lord God, creator and sustainer of the Universe,
we praise you for your faithfulness
and loving kindness towards us.
Before time began you were there, and you have guided and inspired your people throughout all ages.
You do not change, and your compassion never fails us.
Lord, you are far greater than any person or power we can know or imagine.
You do not live in any building made by hands,
your church cannot contain you.
You continually break out and surprise us.
We think we begin to know you
and then you show us another facet of your nature.
Surprising God, we praise you
for the excitement and challenge you bring to our lives!
Grant that we may draw closer to you
in this time of worship. **Amen**

Prayer of Confession

Loving God,
You have invited us to share in your kingdom.
We have received your invitation,
but we confess that we have sometimes made excuses.

For the times when we have been more concerned about what we
are doing at home, school or work:
L: Father: R: **Forgive us**.

For the times when we have been more concerned about what we
have bought, or wish to buy:
L: Father: R: **Forgive us**.

For the times when we have been more concerned about how
others see us than how you see us.
L: Father: R: **Forgive us**.

We confess to you that we are not always the kind of community
you call us to be. We do not love or serve or care for each other
as well as we should, and for that we are sorry. Forgive us in the
name of Jesus Christ and help us to do better in the power of the
Holy Spirit.   **Amen**

Dedication and Commitment   *Possibly following the offering*

Surprising God, your faithfulness and abiding love break through
all the excuses we make, and stir us into action.
Here and now, we dedicate all we have and are, and make a
commitment to love and serve and follow you with no reserve.
Help us to keep our promise.   **Amen**

Blessing

May the faithful God keep us loyal,
may the changeless God keep us secure,
and may the God of surprises keep us
ever alert to new challenges.   **Amen**

3rd Sunday after Pentecost

Presentation

The Old Testament reading reminds us that we should not take God for granted, but remember all that he has done for us; the other two readings stress the authority and power of Jesus Christ. The image of Jesus as the most important stone in the building (Acts) could be used visually. An idea within the gospel is the importance of touch. Always be sensitive when asking people to touch in church – for instance, in the sharing of the peace.

Call to Worship

'The stone which the builders rejected as worthless
turned out to be the most important of all.' (*Ps. 118.22*)
We meet for worship in the power of the name of Jesus Christ of Nazareth, who was crucified and is raised from death. In all the world there is no one else whom God has given who can save us.

Prayers of Thanksgiving and Confession

O God, the Author of Life, we thank you for all the ways in
    which we can experience life through our senses, feelings and
    emotions.
We are sorry for the times when we have not appreciated these
    gifts, or taken them for granted.
L: God, forgive us: R: **And help us to change our ways**.

O God, the great healer, we thank you for all those who help us
    when we are ill or in pain: for doctors and nurses and all who
    support teams in surgeries, clinics and hospitals.
We are sorry for the times when we have not co-operated
    nor been patient with those who try to help us.
L: God, forgive us: R: **And help us to change our ways**.

O God, the Giver of Love, we thank you for your love for us,
    especially as shown by those who love us and care for us; our
    family, relatives and friends.
We are sorry for the times when we have rejected that love and
    hurt those who love us most.
L: God, forgive us: R: **And help us to change our ways**.

O God, Author of Life, great Healer, Giver of Love,
   thank you for touching us, and letting us touch you,
  in daily life, in sickness and in the sharing of love.
We offer these prayers in the powerful name of Jesus.   **Amen**

Meditation

Twelve years
Unable to take her place,
Rejected and cast out . . .
No one could touch her – unclean.
She touched Jesus,
Breaking all the taboos,
And was made well.
'Who touched me?' Jesus said.
She came, afraid,
But left in peace –
Restored.

Twelve years old,
Unable to cross the threshold,
Not eating, and withdrawn . . .
Now she is dying – dead.
Jesus touched her,
Raised her from the bed,
And made her well.
'Give her food,' Jesus said.
Her life returned,
Now she can grow up –
Mature.

Twelve years, or three score years and twelve,
Unable to save ourselves,
Not caring, not loving,
Often tempted – sinners.
Jesus touches us,
Raises us to new life,
Restores us.
'Follow me,' Jesus says.
Our lives changed,
We walk with him,
Redeemed.

Dismissal

Go in peace, your faith makes you whole.
   Go in peace, you grow in Jesus.
      Go in peace, in the power of his name.   **Amen**

4th Sunday After Pentecost

Ezek. 34.1–6
Acts 8.26–38
Luke 15.1–10

Presentation

A 'hide and seek' or 'find but don't tell' game would help in conveying one of today's major themes, that of the lost being found – be it a sheep, coin, or Ethiopian eunuch! The other theme to note (from Ezekiel) is that of caring for the sheep, which are now scattered all over the earth. Articles of shepherding (fleece, lantern, crook) would make a good visual aid for worship. Psalm 23 is useful. This challenge could lead to a positive response by the church to give practical aid to a needy situation.

Call to Worship

L: God, Father of all, you tend and care for us:
R: **We come to worship you**.
L: Jesus, good Shepherd of the sheep, you laid down your
   life for us:
R: **We come to worship you**.
L: Spirit, protector and guide, you inspire and direct us:
R: **We come to worship you**.

Prayer of Confession

Lord, we confess before you that we have not behaved in the way we should. You have shown us the way clearly in Jesus Christ, and we have no excuse.

We have 'consumed the milk' . . . taking from others the things we need to be well-fed and nourished, but with little thought for their needs.
L: In Jesus' name: R: **Please, forgive us**.

We have 'worn the wool' . . . making sure that we are warm and comfortable, well-clothed and housed, and not heeding the plight of the ill-clad and homeless.
L: In Jesus' name: R: **Please, forgive us**.

We have 'slaughtered the fat beasts' . . . thinking little or nothing of the lives of those around us, as long as we get what we want.
L: In Jesus' name: R: **Please, forgive us**.

O Lord, your flock is scattered over all the earth. May we be the
ones to enquire after them and search for them.
May we encourage the weak . . .
   tend the sick . . .
     bandage the injured . . .
       recover the straggler . . .
         search for the lost . . .
And as we have claimed forgiveness in the name of Jesus, may
we also live by his command and in his strength. **Amen**

Meditation on the lost coin

Rejoice with me!
I lost patience, Lord, and became frustrated because
   things took too long, and people kept me waiting.
I lost my temper, Lord, and became angry with those
   who didn't understand what they had done wrong.
I lost my sense of humour, Lord, and was unable to
   laugh or smile at the funny side of situations.
I lost my sense of direction, Lord,
   and started to wander away from your path.
I lost my balance, Lord,
   and wobbled about getting priorities mixed up.
I lost heart, Lord,
   and there seemed no point in the things I tried to do.
But now – rejoice with me!
For with Jesus I can find all those things I have lost!
Thank you, Lord. **Amen**

Prayer after the Bible reading(s)

'Do you understand what you are reading?' asked Philip.
'How can I, without someone to guide me?' said the eunuch.
O God, we thank you that in the church we can hear the good
news of Jesus Christ and have it explained to us. Help us to take
every opportunity we can to reach others, and guide them into
the same knowledge.
In Jesus' name we pray. **Amen**

5th Sunday after Pentecost

Presentation

*People learn from those whose background and culture is different
from their own. Include in worship contributions from other cultures
and races. Sometimes we learn that the priority is to be thankful for
our wholeness, like the Samaritan leper. Objects placed at the front,
with the offering, can symbolize things for which people are thankful
(like spectacles, tablets, hearing aid, photos, etc.).*

Opening Words (*Ruth 1.16*)

'Where you go, I shall go. Where you stay, I shall stay,
Your people will be my people. Your God, my God.'

Thanksgiving Prayer

Everlasting God, we come to you with grateful hearts!
   You created us and all things,
   You love us and look after us,
   Our life is one of blessing.
L: From the bottom of our hearts: R: **We thank you**.

Ever-loving God, we come to you with grateful hearts!
   You have placed us among other people,
   You have set us within different relationships,
   Our life is one of sharing.
L: From the bottom of our hearts: R: **We thank you**.

Ever-caring God, we come to you with grateful hearts!
   You are the source of all our health,
   You bring wholeness into every part of us,
   Our life is one of healing.
L: From the bottom of our hearts: R: **We thank you**.

Ever-listening God, we come to you with grateful hearts!
   Hear our prayers for these things
   For which we are thankful:
Silence

Thank you, everlasting, ever-loving,
  ever-caring, ever-listening God!
L: From the bottom of our hearts: R: **We thank you**.
In Jesus' name.   **Amen**

Prayers of Intercession, based on Kum Ba Ya

All sing 1st verse – Kum Ba Ya
Come by here, Lord, and listen to our prayers.
Come into the lives of all who feel outsiders or rejected by
society. Accept them and us as part of your family.
Come into our lives, and teach us acceptance too.
Silence

All sing 2nd verse – Someone's crying, Lord
Someone's crying, Lord, crying because they are hurt or
depressed, angry or frustrated, lonely or in pain.
Wipe away their tears as you surround them with your love.
Come into our lives, and teach us how to comfort.
Silence

All sing 3rd verse – Someone's praying, Lord
Someone's praying, Lord, praying in anguish and despair,
because their lives seem empty and pointless, and they don't
know where to turn. Hear them and be close to them.
Come into our lives, and teach us to befriend.
Silence

All sing 4th verse – Someone's singing, Lord
Someone's singing, Lord, singing their hearts out with joy and
hope, longing for freedom, or celebrating a special time of
happiness. Sing with them, share their joy and fulfil their hope.
Come into our lives, and teach us to do the same.
Silence

All sing 1st verse again – Kum Ba Ya   **Amen**

Closing Words

Repeat opening words

Go with us now, stay with us now.
We will be your people. You are our God.   **Amen**

6th Sunday after Pentecost

Presentation

Hopelessness and despair can be turned into joy and new life: this is the good news for today! Three stories of 'rescue' in today's lections remind us that one event can sometimes change everything. Link with other rescue stories, especially from charities like RNLI, Christian Aid, Save the Children Fund, NCH etc. Members of the congregation may have a story to share about a time when they were saved.

Opening Words *(Psalm 40.1–3)*

Patiently I waited for the Lord;
he bent down to me and listened to my cry,
He raised me out of the miry pit, out of the mud and clay;
he set my feet on rock, and gave me a firm footing.
On my lips he put a new song, a song of praise to our God.

Prayer *(Using Luke 7.16)*

'God has shown his care for his people.'
Most merciful and caring God,
we pray that you will rescue us.
When, again and again, we fail you in the same ways,
save us from despair.
Silence

'God has shown his care for his people.'
Most merciful and caring God,
we pray that you will rescue us.
When we are worried about others, especially those who are dear to us, help us to be strong for them.
Silence

'God has shown his care for his people.'
Most merciful and caring God,
we pray that you will rescue us.
When we are overwhelmed by our own troubles and anxieties, comfort and support us.
Silence

'God has shown his care for his people'
Most merciful and caring God,
we thank you that at all times of despair, worry and anxiety, you
are close at hand to rescue and save us.
You bring hope and new life, and for that we praise you.   **Amen**

Prayer of Confession   (*Luke 19.9*)

Loving God, you are like a caring parent to us,
    your disobedient children.
We acknowledge that:
– far too often our good intentions let us down,
    but your love is unfailing;
– far too often we do not see beyond the present moment,
    but you perceive the end from the beginning;
– far too often we miss the immediate chance to do good,
    but your goodness is always active.
We ask your forgiveness, in the name of Jesus,
remembering his words:
    'The Son of Man came to seek and to save what is lost.
    Today salvation has come to this house.'
Thanks be to God for our salvation.
Loving God, as we hear your encouraging words and receive
your forgiveness, strengthen us to be your obedient servants.
For Christ's sake.   **Amen**

Offering Prayer

We have received so much from you;
the gift of life, love and salvation.
Nothing we can offer you can ever repay your generosity, but we
bring these gifts as a sign of our gratitude and ask your help to
use them according to your will.   **Amen**

Closing Words

Lord, we have been reminded that you love us,
and that through your Son you have saved us.
We rejoice in his presence with us now and forever.
May those who long for your saving help come to share our joy
as we shout, **'All glory to the Lord!'**   **Amen**

7th Sunday after Pentecost

Presentation

Smell is a sense we rarely use in worship. Use a fragrant candle or perfumed oil burner to back up the story of the woman in Simon's house (a reading which adapts well to drama, especially by adults). Much love was shown here, both to Jesus and by him. The women's selfless actions are unexpected, even shocking. But Jesus is not shocked: he accepts and loves her. Our conduct and behaviour are our own responsibility; we must take the risk of getting involved, and encourage others to do the same.

Call to Worship

May we never tire of doing good . . .
   we shall in due time reap the harvest.
May we work for the good of all . . .
   especially the household of faith.
May we carry one another's burdens . . .
   and in this way fulfil the law of Christ.

Prayer of Praise

Heavenly Father, we come to worship you,
To bring our thanks and praise.
At times like this words seem inadequate.
We only want to rest in your presence, feeling your love around
and within us and letting our love flow back to you.   *Silence*
Thank you for all the gifts,
given for our creation, nurture and enrichment,
but, above all, for the gift of Jesus,
your Son, our Lord, and all that he means to us.
We love you because you first loved us
and showed your love most of all in Jesus.   *Silence*
Accept our worship, Father God,
and accept our thanks and praise, which we offer most sincerely.
  Amen

Meditation

I owed him fifty silver pieces. Just fifty!
He forgave me,
And I love him much.

I owed him five hundred silver pieces. Five hundred!!
He forgave me,
and I love him very much.

I owed him my life in grateful obedience, but I went my own
sinful way.
He forgave me.
And I could never tell you just how much I love him . . .

Prayer for Forgiveness and Offering

Lord, we want to offer you a gift, a sweet-smelling gift, that you
will cherish:
– We offer you our love, yet it is tainted by our
  selfishness and timidity.
  As unworthy as our gift is we offer it in faith and ask
  for your forgiveness.   *Silence*
L: Jesus said: 'Your faith has saved you: go in peace.'
R: **Amen. Thanks be to God**.
– We offer you our time, yet it is tainted by our poor
  stewardship and laziness.
  As unworthy as our gift is we offer it in faith and ask
  for your forgiveness.   *Silence*
L: Jesus said: 'Your faith has saved you: go in peace.'
R: **Amen. Thanks be to God**.
– We offer you our service, yet it is tainted by our
  half-heartedness and inadequacies.
  As unworthy as our gift is we offer it in faith and ask
  for your forgiveness.   *Silence*
L: Jesus said: 'Your faith has saved you: go in peace.'
R: **Amen. Thanks be to God**.

Dearest Lord, as we offer our humble gifts to you, forgive all our
short-comings, accept our love, our time and our service, and
make us fit to serve Christ with our whole lives, in his name.
    Amen

8th Sunday after Pentecost

Presentation

Today's lessons highlight the role of women in God's unfolding purpose. The women who followed Jesus and those who were prominent among the early Christians give good opportunities to explore and celebrate the contribution of women to today's church (Rahab is perhaps a little more problematical!). This would be a suitable Sunday's material for a Women's Anniversary. Information about current women's organizations such as Methodist 'Network', will illustrate and amplify the theme.

Call to Worship

Rejoice in the Lord always, and again I say, rejoice!

Prayer

Dear God, you love us like a mother and a father.
You have given us birth and being.
You have cradled us in your loving arms,
   and nurtured us with good things.
You have watched our first faltering steps,
   and encouraged us to go further.
You have not tied us to your apron-strings,
   but have set us free that we may willingly return.
You always wait to welcome us back
   with the outstretched arms of acceptance.
You comfort us when we are sad or troubled,
   and forgive us when we make mistakes.
You help us to make a fresh start
   and supply what we need for life.
You are so faithful in all your dealings with us
   that we know we can always rely on you.
We are members of your family,
   and we praise you, dear God, mother and father.   **Amen**

For Womankind   *Use two voices*

Voice 1:   We pray for women in many different situations:
Voice 2:   for those who have succeeded where many fail,
Voice 1:   spoken out bravely for equality and justice,
Voice 2:   in spite of being opposed or misunderstood,
Voice 1:   found and followed their vocations
Voice 2:   and served faithfully in church and community.
Voice 1:   For those whose voice is not allowed to be heard,
Voice 2:   who feel owned, used, lacking in identity,
Voice 1:   who feel trapped and unfulfilled, or exploited,
Voice 2:   by their experiences of home-making and child-
bearing,
Voice 1:   who feel excluded by being called 'men',
Voice 2:   who claim to be daughters rather than sons of God.
Voice 1:   Loving and accepting God, support and bless them all,
Voice 2:   your daughters, our sisters, in your world-wide
family.   **Amen**

A Psalm of Praise

Every phrase could have the reponse   **Praise be to God**.

Sing to the Lord a new song:
Let us praise God for the women who have been faithful
servants in every age:
for the mother of Jesus, who loved him and let him go;
for the woman at Jacob's well who recognized Jesus
as the Messiah;
for the women who followed Jesus throughout his ministry;
for the women who cared for him and gave him hospitality;
for the women who watched Jesus die on the cross;
for the women who prepared him for burial
and witnessed his resurrection;
for the women who were leaders in the early church;
for the women who serve faithfully in the church today;
may we look with fresh eyes at the contribution of women
to the church and sing a new song to the Lord.   **Amen**

Dismissal   (*Phil. 4.4*)

Daughters and sons of God, may you be joyful in your lives
together as you share joy in the Lord.
Again I say: all joy be yours.

9th Sunday after Pentecost

I Kings 19.(1–8), 9–21
I Peter 3.13–22
Luke 9.51–62

Presentation

*One theme in the readings is that of God speaking in unexpected ways
– not always communicating in a flamboyant or startling way, but
often in a 'faint murmuring sound', the still, small voice. Use dance/
drama to present this idea. Another theme is that of excuses for not
following Jesus – not only flimsy ones, but heart-felt concerns for
family. This could be up-dated (dramatically) using excuses for not
attending church. A third theme is worrying what people think about
us.*

Opening Words

We could not hear you in the howling wind,
We could not hear you in the crashing earthquake,
We could not hear you in the roaring fire.
   O Lord, we hear you in the still, small voice!
      Come and speak to us now.

Prayer of Forgiveness

   O Lord, why are we here?
We come because we care about you:
   Because we long to serve you, and you alone.
Forgive us when we become disheartened by the reactions of
those around us. Help us to remember that we are not the only
ones who are faithful to you, but that throughout the world
millions belong to you.
   O Lord, why are we here?
We come because we care about you:
   Because we long to serve you, and you alone.
Forgive us when rejection makes us angry and fills us with
vengeance. Help us to remember that people have a choice about
following you, a freedom which is your gift to us.
   O Lord, why are we here?
We come because we care about you:
   Because we long to serve you, and you alone.

Forgive us when we care too much about what others think, and
live in fear of them. Help us to remember that if we are
committed to doing your will, our conscience is clear, and we
need not be ashamed.

O Lord, why are we here?
We come because we care about you:
Because we long to serve you, and you alone.   Amen

Prayer of Discipleship

L: Lord Jesus, we would follow you wherever you go:
R: **Help us not to look back.**
L: We may not be sure what the future holds for us:
R: **Help us not to look back.**
L: We may have other priorities in mind:
R: **Help us not to look back.**
L: We may think we have things to do first:
R: **Help us not to look back.**
L: We may not feel confident or faithful enough:
R: **Help us not to look back.**
L: Looking back may lose us the race, the prize:
R: **Help us not to look back.   Amen**

Meditation

Are you still speaking to us, God? Are you still there?
We are deafened by voices,
opinions, arguments, noise all around,
Why don't you shout at us,
shake us, silence us, make us listen?
Of course, we know it's obvious.
How else would you speak
but in a still, small voice?
And, yes, we have forgotten how to listen.
We can hear you when we try.
In encouraging words from a friend,
In the innocent remarks of a child,
In everyday requests for help,
Even in the silence of the sad and lonely,
we can hear your still, small voice.
Thank you, God, for all the ways in which you do speak to us.
Make our ears sensitive to hear you, and our hearts open to
respond to that still, small voice.

YEAR C

10th Sunday after Pentecost

Ex. 22.21–27
Rom. 12.9–21
Luke 10.25–42

Presentation

Today's lections provide moral and spiritual guidance for Christian living. The gospel passages offer possibilities for part reading, drama, or modern sketches. The parable promoting an active love to neighbours is balanced by Mary listening to Jesus' words, and loving God in him. There is an inseparable link between loving God and loving the people around us. This is amplified in the Romans passage.

An explanation of 'loving ourselves' is needed in order to understand loving 'our neighbours as ourselves'.

Call to Worship

Love the Lord your God with all your heart,
    and with all your soul, and with all your strength,
    and with all your mind, and your neighbour as yourself.

Prayer of Thanksgiving

L: For creating us in your image and for showing us the
    right way to live, O God:
R: **We give you our thanks**.
L: For the gift of Jesus your Son, who taught us about
    the kingdom and how to enter it, O God:
R: **We give you our thanks**.
L: For your Holy Spirit, who enables us to love without
    reserve and to serve without expecting any reward,
    O God:
R: **We give you our thanks**.
L: For inviting us to live in your kingdom, O God:
R: **We give you our thanks.   Amen**

Prayer of Confession

Lord God, you have made us in your image.
Yet we find it hard to love ourselves.
There are so many times we fail you,
there are so many ways in which we could improve.

92

There are so many things we do not like about ourselves.
Please forgive us.   *Silence*
Accept us as we are and help us to become more like you.
Then we may love you with all our heart, with all our soul,
with all our strength, and with all our mind,
and our neighbours as ourselves.

Good Samaritans   *Quick-fire, two voices or a leader and group*

A man was on his way from Jerusalem to Jericho
when he was set upon by robbers, who stripped and beat him up
and went off leaving him half dead.
   Go and do as they did? **No way!**
A priest passed by on the other side.
   Go and do as he did?   **Not likely!**
A Levite passed by on the other side.
   Go and do as he did?   **Not me!**
A Samaritan stopped to help.
   Go and do as he did?   **Yes!**
Because if I don't, that man will die.
What if there had been no one prepared to help?
A missing Samaritan – what then?
Silence
Lord, you have shown us the way to eternal life. If I'm not
prepared to help, then I am not following that way.

Offering Prayer

Because we love you, Lord, and because we want to show our
   love for our neighbour, we bring our gifts.
Because we want the whole world to share in the joy of knowing
   you as God, we bring ourselves.
Accept our offerings and keep us in your love,
for Christ's sake.   **Amen**

Dismissal

Let hope keep you joyful, in trouble stand firm, persist in prayer.
Love in all sincerity, loathing evil and holding fast to the good.
And may grace, peace and mercy follow you all the days of your
life, for Christ's sake.   **Amen**

11th Sunday after Pentecost

Presentation

When will it be? The readings concentrate on waiting expectantly for the day when all will be revealed. Stories like Papa Panov (Martin the Cobbler) may help all ages to understand this idea. Some people may be willing to share their experience (albeit unfortunate and unpleasant) of having been burgled. If they had known when it was going to happen, it might have been prevented.

Call to Worship   (*I Thess. 1.3–4*)

Grace to you and peace.
Your faith has shown itself in action, your love in labour,
your hope in perseverance.
My dear friends . . . God has chosen you.
Let us worship God, in the power of the Holy Spirit.

Prayer of Adoration and Confession   (*Ezek. 12.23*)

The Lord says: 'The days are near
when every vision will be fulfilled.'

Lord God, eternal and all-powerful,
we bow in worship before you.
You existed before all that has ever been,
you are with us in this present time,
you go before us into the unknown future.
We praise you for your devotion to us, your people,
and for the way we can know your love for us.
Forgive us when we are small-minded,
short-sighted, and scornful of the vision of others.
May we know that your word will not be delayed,
that whatever you say will be done.
For the days are near when every vision will be fulfilled.
Give us confidence, we pray, in your promises.   **Amen**

Prayer of Expectant Waiting

L: Lord Jesus, we are waiting for you to return:
R: **Let us be ready to greet you**.
We are like servants, waiting for our master to return from the
wedding party. How easy it is to fall asleep in our comfortable
lives, and forget those whom we could be serving. Instead, help
us to be watchful and alert for those who need us, trying to be
servants of all.
L: Lord Jesus, we are waiting for you to return:
R: **Let us be ready to greet you**.

We are like householders, coming home to find we have been
burgled. How easy it is to be complacent about our lives and not
keep our eyes fixed on your Kingdom. Instead, help us to seek
every opportunity to serve others, whenever there is need.
L: Lord Jesus, we are waiting for you to return:
R: **Let us be ready to greet you**.

How happy you would be to return home and find us working
    for peace and justice, love and comfort.
How happy you would be to return home and find us at the
    door waiting to welcome you.
Help us always to be ready to serve you and prepared for
    your home-coming.
For Christ's sake.   **Amen**

Offering Prayer   (*Luke 12.48*)

Lord, we reflect on your words:
    'Where someone has been given much, much will be
    expected of him; and the more he has had entrusted
    to him the more will be demanded of him.'
Help us, as we offer these gifts, to be generous not only with our
money but also with our love.
In Jesus' name.   **Amen**

Blessing

May the Lord bless you and keep you in his love,
as you serve him in the world
and wait expectantly for his coming in glory.   **Amen**

12th Sunday after Pentecost

Amos 5.18–24
James 1.19–27
Luke 13.(1–9) 10–17

Presentation

The Amos passage epitomizes the message of the prophet: lip-service alone is no good; God requires justice and righteousness. The epistle has shades of Snow White and use of that fairy-tale may help understanding. The gospel lesson, the parable of the fig tree, suggests the possibility of getting a second chance. This can be shared with a story or true life experience.

Call to Worship *(Amos 5.24)*

'Let justice flow on like a river
and righteousness like a never-failing torrent.'

Prayer for Forgiveness

Father God, we thank you for this new day.
Forgive us for all the pain and sorrow
we have caused you and others during the past week.
As you forgive us, change us
and put a loving spirit in us.
We look forward to your new day,
the Day of the Lord.
May it hold for us
light and not darkness, joy and not sorrow.
May our worship be heartfelt, our actions sincere,
and our offerings full of meaning.
May justice and righteousness flow in and through us,
to make us whole again. For your love's sake.   **Amen**

Prayer for Healing   *To follow the gospel*

Loving and compassionate God,
we bring our prayers for suffering people everywhere:
   for sick societies and disabled nations, where people
   are warped by the fear of violence, abuse or crime.
L: Heal us, heal us today: R: **Heal us, Lord Jesus**.
We bring our prayers for suffering people everywhere:

for those we know who are bent over by illness, and
    especially for . . .
L: Heal us, heal us today: R: **Heal us, Lord Jesus**.
We bring our prayers for suffering people everywhere:
    for those crippled by mental distress or disability,
    for those bereaved, depressed or anxious . . .
L: Heal us, heal us today: R: **Heal us, Lord Jesus**.
We pray for ourselves and all who need healing and wholeness
that we may be able to stand up straight and know your power
and presence with us.
L: Heal us, heal us today: R: **Heal us, Lord Jesus**.
Lord Jesus, who healed on the Sabbath day, be with us and with
all for whom we pray, today and every day.   **Amen**

Meditation in front of a mirror   (*Based on James 1*)

'Mirror, mirror on the wall,
    who is the fairest of them all?'
Of course, Lord, I like to think I am.
I glance into my mirror,
check the face nature gave me, then go away
and promptly forget what I look like!
I only want to see the good things,
and not notice the bad.
That's human nature – please forgive me.
James wrote
    'Everyone should be quick to listen,
    slow to speak, and slow to be angry.
    Accept the message, with its power to save you.
    Look into the perfect law.'
'The perfect law' – when I look into that mirror
and do not turn away, but act upon it,
then I will know true happiness.
And maybe then I shall be able to reflect
something of the glory of Christ in my life.
Do help me, Lord!

Closing Words

You have given us another chance to bear fruit,
You have given us another chance to stand up straight,
You have given us another chance to obey your law.
May each one of us give you another chance
to work a miracle in our lives.   **Amen**

13th Sunday after Pentecost

Presentation

*'Keep Sunday special' has been topical and an emotive issue. All
three readings mention the Sabbath – a day kept special, to refresh
ourselves and those with us (even animals). Some people have to
work on Sundays for our good, others find their jobs at risk because
they choose not to work. The story of Eric Liddell (Chariots of Fire)
is a good illustration of faith coming first.*

Call of Worship

L: This is the day that the Lord has made:
R: **Let us rejoice and be glad in it**.

Prayer of Worship

Thank you, God, for Sunday, our special day of celebration!
Sunday is our worship day,
    the day when God began the work of creation;
Sunday is our worship day,
    when Jesus rose from the dead;
Sunday is our worship day,
    the day when the Spirit came;
Sunday is our worship day,
    the first day of a new week.
Thank you, God, for Sunday, our special day of celebration!
Help us to use it to praise you;
– rejoicing in the gifts of your creation,
– celebrating Jesus and the new life he brings,
– renewing ourselves with your Spirit,
– seeking refreshment for the week ahead.
Thank you, loving God, for the gift of Sunday.   **Amen**

Prayer for Time

Lord, we need more time!
Our lives are busy: we have no time for others.
We have no time for you. Life is all a rush.
Silence

But we have time – time to rest in you.
And we have Sunday – a day of rest:
R: **Help us to use it well**.

Lord, we need more time!
We fail to look at other people's circumstances fairly and judge
them hastily and harshly.
Silence
But we have time – time to think, time to act tolerantly.
And we have Sunday – a day of challenge:
R: **Help us to use it well**.

Lord, we need more time!
We forget that, because Christ died and lives again, if we live we
live to the Lord, and if we die we die to the Lord.
Silence
But we have time – a life-time.
And we have Sunday – a day for re-creation:
R: **Help us to use it well**.
Be with us, Lord, to the end of time.   **Amen**

Prayer of Intercession

Lord of time and eternity, we take time,
on our day of rest, to remember the needs of others:
we remember the many people for whom today is not special but
like any other day, a day of work and responsibilities.
We pray:
   –   for those whose responsibilities never vary,
       as they care for families, for neighbours, for . . .;
   –   for those whose work is so demanding that, without this
       day of rest, they could not face another week;
   –   for those who must work on Sundays because it is
       essential to our lives that they do so.
Sustain the life of every community so that all people may find
peace and happiness and know your presence with them. Then
together we may work for your kingdom.   **Amen**

Dismissal

Lord, if we live, we live for you,
if we die, we die for you.
Living or dying, we belong to you, today and forever.   **Amen**

YEAR C

14th Sunday after Pentecost

Presentation

*One theme running through the readings is that of the humble and
exalted. Proverbs and Luke say it is better to start low down and be
raised up higher than vice versa. Perhaps this can be shown visually
for instance, with the seats in church (don't offend the back row!).
Paul speaks of humbling himself, but he also warns against those
who masquerade as apostles or angels of light. Masks would make a
good visual image. Do we let others see us as we really are? Can we
serve people unconditionally, with no thought of glory for ourselves?*

Call to Worship   (*Prov. 25.2*)

'The glory of God is to keep things hidden,
but the glory of kings is to fathom them.'
O God, we come together in church to praise you for your glory
and to learn to understand your eternal Word.

Prayer of Praise

God of the highest heaven and the deepest earth,
   we come before you with our praises.   *Silence*
   You are greater than we can know or imagine,
   and yet you came down to be one with us.
L: Holy and exalted God: R: **We humbly worship you**.
God of purity, pure as fine silver and gold,
   we come before you with our confession.   *Silence*
   You set high standards for our lives. We confess we
   have not lived up to them and need your forgiveness.
L: Holy and exalted God: R: **We humbly worship you**.
God of honour, dignity and worth,
   we come before you with prayers of petition.   *Silence*
   You have given us a place as your children, but we have
   abused our privileges, and need your help.
L: Holy and exalted God: R: **We humbly worship you**.
Exalted, pure and honourable God,
   by your love you lift us up to be with you in your
   kingdom, even though we little deserve that high place.
   Thank you for raising us to new life in you.   **Amen**

A Masked Meditation   *Speakers wearing masks*

Voice 1:   We all wear masks, Lord.
They hide what we are really like,
they protect and reassure us,
they distance us from those we meet.

Voice 2:   But when do we take our masks off?
If we really want to meet people, talk to them, know
them properly and let them know us,
we must be able to take them off.

Voice 3:   Lord, you know us inside out.
No matter what masks we wear, we cannot hide away
from you behind our disguises.
Help us to take our masks off.

Voice 4:   Neither let us pretend to be what we are not,
nor try to be what we cannot.
May we be genuine followers of Christ,
whom people can trust
because we hide nothing from them.

All: Without our masks, (*remove masks*)
we can truly reflect your love.

Prayers of Intercession

Most loving God, we offer our prayers for other people.
We pray for those brought low by difficult situations,
   particularly those who find it a struggle even to exist.
L: Risen Lord: R: **Hear our prayer**.
We pray for those brought low by violence and aggression,
   caught up in wars or conflict not of their own making.
L: Risen Lord: R: **Hear our prayer**.
We pray for those brought low by illness in body or mind,
   especially those we know, . . .
L: Risen Lord: R: **Hear our prayer**.
And we pray for ourselves, that we may serve with no
   thought of glory, praise or even recognition, knowing
   that true happiness comes from doing your will.
L: Risen Lord: R: **Hear our prayer.   Amen**

YEAR C

15th Sunday after Pentecost

Presentation

If you are committed to a great cause, you have to be prepared to lose something, to leave people and things behind – and this can be painful. In the New Testament the 'great cause' is the gospel, related by Paul to the cross and new creation. The cross needs to be a prominent image today. The gospel passage needs some explanation but also supplies ideas which can be taken up in discussion.

Call to Worship

L: The Lord is here!   R: **The Spirit is with us!**
L: We rejoice in hope!   R: **The Spirit is with us!**
L: We unite in worship!   R: **The Spirit is with us!**

Prayer of Thanksgiving and Confession

Generous God, like a loving parent, you provide richly for us, and we are glad to show our gratitude.

Remembering the beauty and wonder of creation,
    all the things which amaze and delight us,
L: We want to say: R: **Thank you, God**.
Remembering the mystery and intricacy of our bodies, and
    the senses through which we enjoy the world around us,
L: We want to say: R: **Thank you, God**.
Remembering the people who love and care for us,
    our relations, friends and neighbours,
L: We want to say: R: **Thank you, God**.
Remembering the teaching, healing and encouragement
    of Jesus, and new life which he makes possible,
L: We want to say: R: **Thank you, God**.

Forgive us when we take your gifts for granted, and accept our thanks for all the precious gifts, that you generously provide for us to enjoy.   **Amen**

Meditation on the Uses of Salt

Are we worth our salt?
Salt enhances flavour and taste. Flavourless salt is fit for nothing,
not even for fertilizer.
Do we add something to the life of our community?
Time to think
Salt removes impurities, leaches out bitterness, but also preserves
and resists decay.
Do we make people's lives more palatable, less bitter?
Time to think
Salt holds a colour dye in cloth, remains behind when snow melts
or water evaporates.
Do we have that staying power, keeping on when others would
give up?
Time to think
Salt raises the freezing point and helps ice to melt.
Do we bring the warmth of love to chilly situations and cool
relationships?
Time to think
Salt aids buoyancy, helping us to float in the sea.
Do we hold up those who are sinking with the weight of anxiety
or despair?
Time to think
Salt is nature's healer, as an antiseptic, soothing sores.
Do we help the healing and recovery of people bruised and
wounded in body or spirit?
Time to think
What good is salt that has lost its saltiness?
Are we worth our salt?

Offering Prayer

Lord Jesus, we bring our offering to you. We want to love you
more than anything else, more even than our own life.
We want to carry our cross and follow you. Help us to set aside
everything that keeps us from you and to fix our eyes on your
offering of yourself for us on the cross.
As we offer our money, we offer ourselves in worship and
service. Accept, then, these gifts and ourselves, in love.   **Amen**

16th Sunday after Pentecost

Presentation

*Clothing, especially coats, figures prominently in today's lessons;
special coats given with affection (Genesis and Luke) and
the symbolic garments which are the Christian ways of behaving
(Colossians). A 'technicolour dreamcoat', painted, made as a collage
or borrowed from a theatrical costumiers could be a visual focus.
Joseph and the Prodigal Son could easily be dramatized (or use a
modern version). Both stories reveal the resentment of the elder
brother(s) – whereas tolerance and forgiveness are Christian virtues.*

Call to Worship   (*Ps. 107.1*)

'It is good to give thanks to the Lord,
for his love endures for ever.'

Prayer of Confession

Loving and forgiving God,
we make our confession before you.
You have shown us, through the scriptures,
the qualities in which we should be clothed,
if we want to be seen as Christians.
We come before you covered in shame at our shabbiness
and ask you to forgive us.
Forgive us when we have not shown compassion, kindness,
    gentleness and patience.
Forgive us when we have held grudges, grumbled about
    suffering, and cared only about how the world sees us.
Forgive us when we have forgotten Jesus' teaching,
    or forgotten to live by it and share it.
Reclothe us in our rightful minds.
Wrap us up in your love and keep us in Christ's peace.
May the gospel enrich us and fill us with wisdom.
And may we always be thankful, singing our hymns of worship
with joy and gratitude for all we have received.
In the name of the Lord Jesus, through whose power we speak
and act to the glory of God the Father.   **Amen**

Meditation 1

Voice 1: Lord it's not fair!
Why should he get special treatment?
I've been doing my duty for ages,
and I've had no special reward.
It's not fair!
Why should she get welcomed back?
I've been here all the time
and you haven't celebrated that.
It's just not fair!

Voice 2: My child, my son, my daughter.
Who said anything about being fair?
Was what happened to my son, Jesus, fair?
You and I are very close,
and everything I have is yours.
We celebrate because he who was dead
has come back to life.
That is the measure of my love for you.

Meditation 2

Joseph was given a coat, a long-sleeved garment of legendary 'many colours'.
  It was a sign of his father's affection.
  But it caused jealousy and resentment.
The younger son was given a coat, the finest robe in the house, along with shoes and a ring.
  It was a sign of honour, a welcome home.
  But it caused jealousy and resentment.
The Christian is given a coat, part of a whole suit of clothes to fit one of God's chosen people.
  It is a gracious gift, given in love.
  It should inspire tolerance and forgiveness.
Lord, help us to wear our garments with joy,
but also with humility.
May we never appear unsuitably dressed in your presence.

Dismissal

Remember what Jesus taught,
let his words enrich your lives and make you wise.
And then you will go with God's blessing,
and wear the truly colourful clothes of a Christian life.

17th Sunday after Pentecost

Presentation

Powerful issues such as greed, love of money, and good stewardship are often hard to grapple with, yet they are a major part of our Christian teaching. Use balance scales as a focus for worship.

Activities or stories which show cheating, short measure or inaccurate weighing would help illustrate the readings. Wesley's sermon on the 'Use of Money', advising that we gain, save and give all we can, will show these are not only modern ideas.

Call to Worship   *(Ps. 23.1)*

'The Lord is my Shepherd, I lack for nothing.'
Let us worship the Lord who gives us all we need for life.

Prayer of Confession   *This could be used responsively*

Voice 1:   God of all nations and Father of all people,
　　　　　 forgive us for our blindness and complacency in a
　　　　　 world where your gifts are so unfairly divided.
Voice 2:   **The love of money is the root of all evil.**

Voice 1:   Forgive us when we are defensive about our love of
　　　　　 money, and ignore your challenge to look at ourselves
　　　　　 and our giving.
Voice 2:   **The love of money is the root of all evil.**

Voice 1:   Forgive us when, all too easily, we let money and
　　　　　 possessions become gods for us and we are greedy to
　　　　　 have more.
Voice 2:   **The love of money is the root of all evil.**

Voice 1:   Forgive us when, for the love of money, we hurt and
　　　　　 reject those who ask for the little they need just to
　　　　　 stay alive.
Voice 2:   **The love of money is the root of all evil.**

Voice 1:   Jesus said: 'You cannot serve God and money.'
God our Father, we want to serve you alone. Help us
to feel so secure in our love for you that we do not
need to put our faith in possessions. We ask it in
Jesus' name, who was rich but for our sake became
poor. **Amen**

Prayer of Intercession

Different voices could read each paragraph

Let us remember those with swollen bellies and matchstick limbs
who have no food today,
while we look forward to another good meal.
Silence

Let us remember those with cast-off clothes who feel lucky to
have an outfit of rags,
while we choose the latest fashion garments in the shops.
Silence

Let us remember those with only a cardboard box for a home,
who live in slums or shanty towns,
while we improve our already more than adequate houses.
Silence

Let us remember those begging on the streets, who live on credit
and die in debt,
while we work out better investments for our savings.
Silence

God of justice and equality, the prophets told us how you react
when the scales are tipped against the poor.
May we too see the way to effective action and, with your help,
bring help to the poorest of the poor. **Amen**

Offering Prayer

We brought nothing into this world,
and we can take nothing out.
You, Lord, have made us stewards of all we possess.
May we prove trustworthy in handling our material wealth,
so that we may be trusted with the riches of heaven. **Amen**

18th Sunday after Pentecost

Presentation

Life-styles are once more addressed in today's challenging readings, and the divide between rich and poor is high-lighted. Is God 'biased' to the poor and is priority given to those whose needs are greatest? The way we treat people when we know about their wealth or status is examined. The parable of the rich man and Lazarus is ideal for dramatization using either the biblical account or a modern version.

Call to Worship

Psalm 145 verses 1–6, used responsively.

Prayer of Confession *Using two voices, at the front and back of the church, or responsively.*

Gracious God, we thank you for all the richness of creation.
We live in a green and fertile country,
and pleasant sights and sounds surround us – grass and
flowers, blossom and trees, rivers and lakes.
We pray for those who know only rock and sand, dry and parched, and see no running water.

Gracious God, we thank you for our material riches.
We enjoy nourishing and interesting food,
nice homes and many possessions.
We pray for those who trek across deserts to reach what they call food and own only the rags they stand in.

Gracious God, we thank you for our spiritual riches.
We have comfortable lives with time to debate the way
to eternal life. We have books, music, art and
religious teaching to stimulate our minds and help us
in our search for you.
We pray for those whose lives are spent just surviving another day.

We thank you for all that we have.
Help us not to be blind and deaf to the needs of others.

Lord, this is our prayer.
Help us to know and do your will.   Amen

Offering Prayer

Father, we dedicate our gifts to you,
   asking that this money may be used wisely in worship,
   service and evangelism.
Father, we dedicate our lives to you,
   asking that you will use us to serve others without
   thought for ourselves.
In Jesus' name.   **Amen**

Meditation

 Am I really a Christian at all?

When I show favouritism to those who have money,
when I try to impress those with status,
and ignore or humiliate those with neither . . .
   Am I really a Christian at all?

When I eat lavishly with guests at my table,
when I spend freely and dress splendidly,
and ignore or humiliate the poor on my doorstep . . .
   Am I really a Christian at all?

Lord, if I really had known who you were!
If I had recognized that those without money can be rich in faith
and will possess your promised kingdom . . .
Although you have risen from the dead,
I have failed to take heed, failed to be warned.
   I wonder sometimes, am I really a Christian at all?

Dismissal

Love your neighbour as you love yourselves.
Give to the poor from the riches given to you.
Serve God and save yourselves.

19th Sunday after Pentecost

Presentation

'Don't take advantage of someone when they are down' is the message in Leviticus. God rescued the Israelites from slavery, and they must not enslave others. Servants and slaves also feature in Luke and Philemon. In the latter, the runaway slave Onesimus would make a good subject for a role-play interview. We need to find the right balance between self-esteem and humility as we serve God in others. Woe betide us if we create a stumbling block to another's faith.

Call to Worship *(Philemon 3)*

'Grace to you and peace from God our Father
and the Lord Jesus Christ!'

Prayer of Adoration

We praise you, O God, for setting your people free:

You freed the Israelites from slavery in Egypt and led
 them safely across the wilderness to the Promised Land.
You established your Covenant with them at Sinai and gave
 them the Commandments as a guide to life.
You freed them again from slavery in Babylon and returned
 them to Jerusalem, the holy city, and to the Temple.
You promised them a New Covenant, joining you to them and
 them to you, freeing them to know you as Lord.
You sent your Son, Jesus, to deliver us all from the slavery
 of sin and lead us to the eternal life of heaven.
You set us free from slavery to the Law,
 establishing the New Covenant with his blood.
You fill us with your Holy Spirit, releasing us from self-
 interest to live in your service and the service of others.

We praise you, O God,
for giving us the freedom to worship and serve you. **Amen**

Prayer of Confession

O God, our Servant King, we ask your forgiveness:
- for the times when we have taken advantage of other
  people and used their downfall for our benefit.

L: Forgive us: R: **And set us free to serve you**.
- for the times when we have been reluctant to forgive
  and have made others suffer by our stubbornness.

L: Forgive us: R: **And set us free to serve you**.
- for the times when we have not helped others to faith
  and have placed a stumbling-block in their way.

L: Forgive us: R: **And set us free to serve you**.
- for the times when pride and arrogance possess us
  and we seek extra credit for merely doing our duty.

L: Forgive us: R: **And set us free to serve you**.

In silence we ask forgiveness for the times we have not served
God but served ourselves.   *Silence*

O God, the Servant King, hear our prayers.

L: In the name of Christ our sins are forgiven:

R: **Thanks be to God.   Amen**

Prayer of Petition

Loving Master,
You know what it is like to be a servant:
   you served your disciples by washing their feet,
   and you never complained about your work-load.

L: Lord: R: **Help us to do our duty**.

When our lives are busy and full of activity,
   when we come home tired and still have more work to do,
   when we feel we are stretched to the limit.

L: Lord: R: **Help us to do our duty**.

May we not expect praise and congratulations,
   may we be glad to serve you in love and devotion,
   may we be thankful that we can serve you.

L: Lord: R: **Help us to do our duty**.

Loving Master and Lord,
   accept us as your loving servants, and may our duty be
   our delight.   **Amen**

20th Sunday after Pentecost

Presentation

We can be so caught up in the 'daily round and common task' that we fail to see the obvious – we are too busy or too close to notice. The Day of the Lord will come upon us like this. Like falling in love, we will know when it has happened rather than when to expect it. Ask someone to retell an experience of something coming 'out of the blue' and how they made the most of it.

Call to Worship (*Ps. 122.1*)

I rejoiced when they said to me,
'Let us go to the house of the Lord.'
In the house of the Lord, let us rejoice in his presence.

Prayer of Confession

O God, when you see what has happened through the ages, do you regret what you did for us?
We must disappoint you.

Creator God, you created this world, with all its beauty,
   with plants, animals, birds and people.
   It was perfect, but we have spoiled it.
L: Lord, when we disappoint you: R: **We are truly sorry**.

Father God, you sent your only Son to live our life,
   to die our death, and give us the example for living.
   But still we behave in the same old way.
L: Lord, when we disappoint you: R: **We are truly sorry**.

Loving God, you sent your Holy Spirit to guide our lives,
   but we have chosen to live in our way not yours.
   We destroy each other with hatred and violence.
L: Lord, when we disappoint you: R: **We are truly sorry**.

From our heart, we pray that you will forgive us. Accept our confession of failure and confirm our resolve to try and do better. We offer our prayers through Jesus Christ.   **Amen**

Meditation

The Kingdom of God is among you!
No good saying 'Look, here it is' or 'There it is',
No good listening to those who say 'Here', 'There'.
It is everywhere.
Now is the Kingdom of God among you!

Everyone is busy, as in the days of Noah or Lot,
eating, drinking, buying, selling, planting, building,
too busy to notice the day when the Son of Man is revealed.
Now is the Kingdom of God among you!

Leave your belongings, do not turn back home,
beware when sleeping or preparing food, watch out whatever
you are doing.
Now is the Kingdom of God among you!

Like a lightning flash, like a flood or fire,
without warning, without time to prepare, it is coming.
Now is the Kingdom of God among you!

God and King of the Universe,
Make us ready for your Kingdom.
Turn our wisdom and our values upside down
so that we may understand that to gain life we must be prepared
to lose it, for you and for the gospel.   **Amen**

Offering Prayer   (*Based on Phil. 1*)
Thank you, God, for all you have given us;
– for those who work hard for your Kingdom,
– for the deepening of insight and love,
– and for all that we learn by experience.
Then, at the Day of Christ Jesus, may we be flawless and without
blame, yielding the full harvest of righteousness that comes
through him, to the praise and glory of God.

Dismissal

Go in the grace of God, in the love of Jesus,
and in the power of the Spirit, to live and work
for the Kingdom of God which is among you.   **Amen**

21st Sunday after Pentecost

Presentation

Today's readings wrestle with problems which beset the Early Church – can Gentiles become Christians and is it important to keep Jewish rules to be counted as 'righteous'? They stress that it is faith, not ritual, which enables people to be forgiven by God. Zacchaeus is an obvious choice for dramatization. Point out that Zacchaeus is challenged by Jesus, though Jesus gives no verbal challenge to him. Even small people (figuratively as well as literally!) can become great in God's sight, if they keep the Covenant.

Call to Worship   *(Ps. 32.1–2)*

'Happy are those whose lawless deeds are forgiven,
whose sins are blotted out. Happy are those whose sin
the Lord does not count against them.'

Prayer of Adoration

Almighty God, Father of all nations,
We meet together to give you our praise and worship.
   We thank you for our inheritance of faith.
   We are glad to be part of your church and
   we praise you for your continual faithfulness, love and
   care for each of us.
L: You are our God: R: **And we are your people**.

We know that we fall far short of your standards.
   We fail you and let you down so many times.
   It surprises us that, if we turn to you, you are ready to
   forgive us, restore us and reinstate us in your family.
   We do not deserve this, but we are thankful to you.
L: You are our God: R: **And we are your people**.

Throughout all ages you have been faithful and sure.
   You have made a Covenant with us, and we want to affirm
   our intention to keep it.
   We dedicate ourselves to your service, knowing that with
   your help we will be able to live for you.
L: You are our God: R: **And we are your people**.

We offer our prayers in the name of Jesus,
   who lived, and died and rose again for us.   **Amen**

Prayer of Confession

We thank you, Lord, that with all our faults we can come to you
with confidence, not because we keep your law but because we
follow your path of faith.
In silence we acknowledge those things for which we need to be
forgiven.
Silence
Help us, we pray, to remove those barriers within us which still
separate us from you. And grant us, in the name of Christ, the
joy of your forgiveness.   **Amen**

Meditation

'Zacchaeus was a very little man . . .'
Often, Lord, I feel very little before you.
When I hear your invitation to be with you,
   I am ashamed.
I stand accused of many terrible things by others.
   I am sorry.
But you come, and I take another look at myself.
   I am renewed.
I realize that keeping the Covenant depends on my faith.
   I am committed.
I am a child of Abraham, salvation is for me.
   I am saved.
I climb up to see you, but I must climb down again.
   I am to serve.
The Son of Man has come to seek and to save what is lost.
   I was lost, but now I am one of God's chosen!

Closing Words

You are our God and we are your people.
Grant us your blessing as we go out into your world.   **Amen**

22nd Sunday after Pentecost

Presentation

Since the time of the apostles the laying on of hands has been a significant act in the life of the church, and is used today in the reception and confirmation of members as well as the ordination of ministers. In this way, they are all commissioned to share in the handing on of the good news. Illustrate this with a simple game: two lines of people hold hands and stand with their backs to each other, a leader squeezes the hands of those at one end, and the 'message' is passed down the line to the other end, when the message is received that person drops a handkerchief to show that it has been received. Draw out the themes of authority and succession.

Prayer of Adoration

We adore you, living God, Creator, Father and Lord.
   You are mighty, powerful and great,
   and in you is all authority.
L: Living God, we worship you: R: **We adore you**.

We adore you, Jesus Christ, Saviour, Redeemer and Friend.
   You are gracious, kind and compassionate,
   and you have all authority.
L: Jesus Christ, we worship you: R: **We adore you**.

We adore you, Holy Spirit, Enabler, Comforter, and Guide.
   You are the giver and renewer of life,
   and through you comes our authority.
L: Holy Spirit, we worship you: R: **We adore you.** **Amen**

Prayer of Confession   *Could use different voices*

Leader: Heavenly Father, we confess our sins to you:
Voice 1:   We have trusted in ourselves rather than in your
           fatherly goodness.
Voice 2:   We have not understood that it is only with your help
           that we can act, or speak or think as we should.

Voice 3:   We often find it hard to accept authority, and so feel
           rebellious or resentful.
Voice 4:   We often find it hard to exercise authority and to lead
           without being overbearing.
Leader: We ask your forgiveness in the name of Jesus, whose
           authority lay in the perfection of his humble
           service.   **Amen**

Credal Prayer

Almighty God, ruler of all,
we thank you for sending us Jesus, your Son,
to save us from sin and death.
He died on a cross to save the world.
You brought him back to life
and gave him all authority in earth and heaven.
You sent your Holy Spirit upon your church
so that we may live in your way.
We pray for all those in authority,
that they may use their power for good.
Help them to hear the voice of conscience
and not be deaf to the clamour for equality or change.
And we pray for ourselves, remembering that,
under your authority, we have perfect freedom;
and asking that, willingly accepting the yoke of your kingdom, we
may be set free to love and serve.
In Jesus' name.   **Amen**

Prayer of Rededication

Ever-loving God,
we remember with gratitude that we have been welcomed into
Christ's church in baptism and in confirmation have had the
opportunity to commit ourselves to him.
We pray that in this moment, rejoicing in your generous love and
in our fellowship in Christ, we may offer ourselves again to be
affirmed and strengthened by the power of your Holy Spirit:
Silence

Let us go in peace to live and work to God's praise and glory.
Thanks be to God.   Amen

Last Sunday after Pentecost

Judges 7.1–8, 19–23
Heb. 11.32–12.2
Luke 19.11–27

Presentation

Are we prepared to take a risk in faith? Gideon risked losing the battle, following God's orders to use a smaller army. The servant hid his money because he dared not risk losing it and being disgraced. Hebrews lists those who risked everything for God. God risked himself in Christ in order to gain salvation for all. Talk about playing games (such as chess) and being prepared to give up a piece in order to win. Get a long-distance runner to talk about how they prepare for and run a race, giving up an easy life in the hope of winning.

Call to Worship

We are surrounded by a great cloud of witnesses!
Let us throw off everything which hinders us,
especially the sins which hold us back, and run with resolution
the race through life to the goal of heaven.

Prayer of Trust

O God, are we sure enough of your presence with us
   to risk stripping away our selfish security?
   Make us brave enough to risk everything for you.
L: Help us, Lord: R: **To put our trust in you**.

O God, are we sure enough of your presence with us
   to risk losing our material possessions?
   Make us brave enough to risk everything for you.
L: Help us, Lord: R: **To put our trust in you**.

O God, are we sure enough of your presence with us
   to risk losing everything for your sake?
   Make us brave enough to risk everything for you.
L: Help us, Lord: R: **To put our trust in you**.

God, you were willing to risk everything for us when you
   sent your Son, Jesus, to live with us and die for us,
   and you raised him again to new life.

Following his example help us to risk all that we have and all that
we are in your service.   **Amen**

Prayer of Intercession

Heavenly Father,
we thank you for all those who through the ages have kept the
faith and been prepared to take risks for you.

We remember those whose stories are told in the Bible,
    who were miraculously saved and achieved great things.
We remember those who suffered torture and horrific death
    rather than renounce their faith.
We remember those who, today, lead churches in difficult
    circumstances, working in under-developed areas or
    facing persecution and antagonism.
We remember those who are imprisoned for their belief,
    who have risked their liberty and lives because they
    stand for equality, justice and freedom of speech.

Surrounded and encouraged by all these witnesses,
    may we run our race, keeping our eyes fixed on Jesus,
    the pioneer and perfecter of our faith.   **Amen**

Offering Prayer   *(Luke 19.26)*

'I tell you, everyone who has will be given more;
but whoever has nothing will forfeit even what he has.'

Lord, we are grateful for our gifts and talents.
As we offer this money, we offer ourselves
to be used for your kingdom of love.
Help us to increase in faith and love,
giving all that we have for you,
always confident of the joy that lies ahead of us.   **Amen**

Dismissal and Blessing

Go, throw off everything that holds you back from living your life
in praise and service to God, and may the Lord of Life grant you
strength and courage on the journey of faith.   **Amen**

YEAR C

Church Anniversary

Ezek. 43.1–10
I Cor. 12.14–26
Luke 19.41–48

Presentation

The 'church' is both a place dedicated to the worship of God, and a community dedicated to expressing love towards God, one another, and the world. The church building is thus a focus of both worship and fellowship, containing many helpful symbols.

In the prayer of thanksgiving, ask the congregation to turn their attention to various objects around the church.

Call to Worship

We stand on holy ground.
The Lord is in this place.
Let us worship and serve God
with reverence and love,
both here and in the world.

Prayer of Adoration

God of past and present and future,
God of eternity,
we gather here to worship you,
to offer you our praise and thanksgiving,
as did our ancestors in the faith
down through the years.
And we wonder, Lord,
that you can be the same,
yesterday, today and forever;
our parents' and our children's God
as well as ours;
and yet
your love is born anew
in every Christian's heart and life;
your words are spoken afresh
to every generation.

God, we praise you,
for you are truth;
the truth for our lives
today and forever.

120

In the name of Jesus Christ,
the Way, the Truth and the Life.   **Amen**

Prayer of Thanksgiving

At the cross
For the gift of your Son, who died and rose again that we might
be one with you: R: **Loving God, we thank you**.

At the Communion Table
For the gift of the Eucharist, where together we share in his
saving action of love: R: **Loving God, we thank you**.

At the font
For the gift of baptism, the sign and seal that marks us out as
yours alone: R: **Loving God, we thank you**.

At the pulpit or lectern
For the gift of your word, that brings us hope and joy, challenge
and comfort, guidance and peace: R: **Loving God, we thank you**.

At the organ or piano
For the gift of music and all that helps our worship to be
beautiful and sincere: R: **Loving God, we thank you**.

Loving God, we thank you for this, our church. We thank you
for the many times we have felt you close to us in this building –
times of joy and times of sadness. We thank you for the times
when we have heard you speak to us, through words of worship
or fellowship. And, remembering especially those who have died,
we thank you for the friendship, love and concern that we have
found here. Loving God, we thank you for this, our church. In
the name of Christ, the Author of our faith.   **Amen**

Dismissal

Fed by the Bread of Life, refreshed by the word of peace,
emboldened by the Spirit of faith, go out in Christ's name.

Harvest Festival

Gen. 41.1–7, 25–32
Rev. 14.14–18
Luke 12.16–31

Presentation

*All three readings are 'stories': Pharaoh's dream, John's vision and
Jesus' parable. Whatever theme you choose, (and harvest gives
plenty of choice) try and use story-telling as an address.*

Call to Worship

Life is more than food, the body more than clothes.
Set your minds on the kingdom of God and God will provide for
all your needs.
We worship God, the giver of all we need, and focus our
thoughts on the Kingdom of God on earth and in heaven.

Prayer of Confession

Forgive us, generous God, when we forget that the world
　is your creation and take its gifts for granted.
We use water,
　but do not think about your overflowing love;
We eat food,
　but do not let you feed us with your Word;
We wear clothes,
　but do not bother about how we look to you;
We burn fuel,
　but do not let you warm our hearts with your love.

Generous God, we are sorry for ignoring your hand in the things
we take and use for our comfort and pleasure.
We ask your forgiveness for our complacency, for thinking we
can manage the world and its resources without you.
May we not store up your gifts without giving thanks but use
them wisely for ourselves and for others.

Generous God, in the name of Christ, forgive us.
Set us free from our worries, knowing that you provide for our
needs and will guide us in the ways of your kingdom.　**Amen**

Prayer of Petition

Joseph knew the meaning of Pharaoh's dream and used his
  knowledge to provide for the people in their need.
May we use our knowledge of nature and science wisely to
provide food for everyone.

Jesus challenged the crowd with a parable about riches, asking
  what was most important in life – food or faith?
May we seek nothing more in life than to be faithful in our
worship and service for the glory of God's Kingdom.

John the Divine had a vision of a new earth filled with Christ's
  disciples, a rich harvest for God.
May we use our lips and lives to share the good news about Jesus
and challenge others to join us,
confident that God's kingdom will come.   **Amen**

Offering Prayer

We offer these fruits of harvest in thanksgiving
  for your faithfulness in creation.
We offer this money in thanksgiving
  for your generous gifts to us.
We offer ourselves in thanksgiving
  for all that faith in Christ enables us to be.
May each of these offerings be used by your church
  to bring a rich harvest for your Kingdom.   **Amen**

Dismissal

God who feeds the birds of the air, feeds you.
God who clothes the grass of the field, clothes you.
God who promises all who follow the gift of eternal life,
  blesses you with love.
Go in faith, set your minds on his kingdom, and all you need will
come to you through the generosity of God.
R: **Thanks be to God.   Amen**

Material for Year D

9th Sunday before Christmas

Presentation

*The God who spoke creation into being is the God we have come to
know in Jesus Christ, the Word of God. 'Word' and 'light' are two
key words in the readings. Light a large candle during the Genesis
reading and surround it with objects and pictures representing
humankind, animals, fish, plants etc. During the John reading, place
a Bible, open at John 1, in front of the candle.*

Call to Worship

Voice 1: In the beginning God
created the heavens and the earth.
Voice 2: God said 'Let there be light.'
And God saw the light was good.
Voice 1: Come, let us worship the Author of the Universe:
Voice 2: Who makes something out of nothing;
Voice 1: Who makes light out of darkness;
Voice 2: Who loves and watches over the whole of creation.

Meditation

God has created us in his image.
Male and female:
Our fatherly, motherly God has created us
in his or her image.
Black and white,
The God in whom we live and move and have our being
has created us
in his image.
Young and old:
Our eternal, unchanging, ever-new God has created us
in her image.
We have been created in the image of God:
to know God;
to love God;
to care for all that God has made.

Prayer

Creator God,
Your world is full of darkness.
We have blackened the waters with oil.
We have darkened the heavens with fumes.
We have burnt down the forests
and plundered and squandered
what you gave us in trust.
L: Lord, speak light into our darkness:
R: **Lord, let there be light**.

Creator God,
Your world is full of darkness.
Sorrow clouds the faces of the suffering.
The sad and anxious feel their way through the gloom.
We struggle through dark and difficult times
and the shadow of death
looms over us all.
L: Lord, speak light into our darkness:
R: **Lord, let there be light**.

Creator God,
Your world is full of darkness.
Our lives are dismal with selfishness,
overcast by guilt and despondency.
Deeds of darkness,
violence, abuse, neglect,
threaten and destroy.
L: Lord, speak light into our darkness:
R: **Lord, let there be light**.

In the name of Christ, the light of the world,
whom the darkness cannot overcome.   **Amen**

Dismissal

Let the light of Christ shine in your hearts.
Let the light of Christ shine through your lives.
Let the light of Christ shine throughout the world.

8th Sunday before Christmas

Presentation

Humankind proves unable to resist the temptation to disobey God.
Mime the Genesis reading. Ask the congregation why Eve acted as
she did. Can they identify with her motives?

Call to Worship

'God so loved the world
that he gave his only Son
that everyone who has faith in him
may not perish but have eternal life.'
Come, let us proclaim our living faith
and claim the love of our Creator God.

Meditation

The apple shone among the leaves,
Glinting in the sunlight.
The new-made world smelt soft and fresh.
All was relaxed,
Nothing to strive for,
Totally laid back.

The apple glinted like a knife
Just out of reach on a table-top.
'Don't touch, child Adam, child Eve,
That hard, sharp knife,
Though of infinite use,
Can cut and scar and maim.'

The apple shone among the leaves.
Its radiance burnt into their hearts;
Its fragrance excited their every thought.
Child Eve reached up,
Picked it, ate it.
And it was very sharp.

Prayer of Confession

Loving God, when we know what we should not do,
  but cannot stop ourselves from doing it:
L: Forgive us: R: **And strengthen us**.

Loving God, when we know what we should do,
  but feel incapable of doing it:
L: Forgive us: R: **And strengthen us**.

Loving God, when we are blind to the needs of those
  around us and only look to satisfy our own:
L: Forgive us: R: **And strengthen us**.

Loving God, when we are deaf to your voice,
  preferring to listen to other voices:
L: Forgive us: R: **And strengthen us**.

Gracious God,
  Through Christ you forgive us,
  By your Spirit you strengthen us.
  We turn to you and dedicate ourselves
  to following your way of love.   **Amen**

Offering Prayer

Generous God,
  Out of love you created all that is;
  Out of love you created humankind;
  Out of love you save us from the consequences of our sin.
  Out of love, we offer you these gifts;
  Out of love, we offer you ourselves.
Accept them and us, in the name of the second Adam,
your Son, Jesus Christ.   **Amen**

Blessing

God, the Creator, fill you with joy.
God, the Redeemer, fill you with hope.
God, the Comforter, fill you with peace.
And the blessing of God, Father, Son and Holy Spirit,
be with you, now and evermore.   **Amen**

7th Sunday before Christmas

Presentation

Abraham's relationship of faith with God was expressed in his willingness to journey into the unknown. Put up a map and mark where members of the congregation have been on holiday. Talk about the journeys they have made, and their feelings about them. Compare with the journey of faith. Read the Romans passage immediately after that from Genesis.

Call to Worship

Wherever our father Abraham travelled he built an altar to worship God. We, too, are travelling on the journey of life.
Let us, like him, offer sacrifices of praise to the God who travels with us.

Prayer of Adoration

Loving God,
wherever we are, wherever we go,
you are there.
You created the world
to be our home
and our place of journeying.
Your glory shines through the world
and yet far transcends it.
Loving God,
we praise you,
Creator of the World.

Loving God,
wherever we are, wherever we go,
you are there.
You sent your only Son
to be our guide,
our companion and our saviour.
Your love shines through his life.
Your love has conquered death.
Loving God,
we praise you,
Father of our Lord Jesus Christ.

Loving God,
wherever we are, wherever we go,
you are there.
You have sent your Holy Spirit
to warm our hearts,
to challenge and encourage us.
Your power shines through your people.
Your power unites them in love.
Loving God,
we praise you,
Giver of the Holy Spirit.

Prayers of Intercession

Ever-living God, there are many mountains that obstruct the long
   road to your kingdom:
For the nations of the world, there are mountains of injustice,
   oppression, exploitation and warfare.
L: Lord, give us the faith to remove mountains:
R: **Keep us travelling the road towards you**.
For the people of the world, there are mountains of indifference,
   violence, hatred and greed.
L: Lord, give us the faith to remove mountains:
R: **Keep us travelling the road towards you**.
For the church in the world there are mountains of disunity,
   apathy, materialism, lack of vision.
L: Lord, give us the faith to remove mountains:
R: **Keep us travelling the road towards you.   Amen**

God, the First and the Last, we each encounter many mountains
on our journey towards you. Some we must climb and claim for
you. Others will be removed, if we can truly trust in you. We
pray for ourselves and for all those with mountains to climb,
whether of illness, bereavement, anxiety or depression. Lord,
give us the faith that keeps us journeying on towards you.
In the name of our companion, Jesus Christ.   **Amen**

6th Sunday before Christmas

Presentation

*Small acts of love all play a part in God's plan of salvation.
Dramatize the Exodus reading, explaining the background to it and
the consequences of Moses' rescue. Ask the congregation to draw
comparisons between this story and the Christmas story. Follow the
discussion with the New Testament readings.*

Call to Worship

We are not slaves but free people.
We are not servants but God's own children.
Come, let us worship our living, loving God
with the joy and delight that freedom brings.

Prayer of Praise

God of creation,
we praise you,
for you made the world
to be our home.

God of salvation,
we praise you,
for you rescue us
from our sins.

God of Abraham,
we praise you,
for you promise us
our faith is well-founded.

God of Moses,
we praise you,
for you set us free
and guide our lives.

God in Christ,
we praise you,
through you the world was made,

through you we find salvation,
through you we come to faith,
through you we learn the way of love.

God in Christ,
we praise you,
we worship and adore you. **Amen**

Prayer of Petition

Moses' mother gave birth to him, loved him, hid him away. She
let him go, protecting him as well as she could, when it seemed
his only chance of life.
Lord, we pray that we may provide a good start for the children
among us. Teach us how to truly love, cherish and protect. Show
us when it is time to let them go.
May they, helped by our example, come to live life in you.

Pharaoh's daughter heard a baby cry among the rushes. Moved
to pity, she rescued the child and cared for him.
Lord, we pray that we may be moved to pity by the cries of your
unhappy children. Teach us to act on our loving impulses, to help
alleviate the distress caused by hunger, sickness and cruelty.

Moses' sister watched over the baby, weighed up the situation
and used her wits to ensure that Moses was reunited with his
mother.
Lord, we pray that we may learn to use the gifts you have given
us in wise and loving ways. Teach us the skills of watching and
listening and help us to find the right words to say.

Lord, you used the ordinary emotions, actions and words of three
women long ago to further your plan to save creation. We pray
that you will use us, too, in the building of your kingdom of love.
In Jesus' Name. **Amen**

5th Sunday before Christmas

Presentation

Jesus Christ is King of kings, but his is the kingdom of God, of righteousness and truth. Ask the congregation either to suggest and write up the names of powerful people, or to paste up pictures of them. Above, write JESUS CHRIST – KING OF KINGS. Discuss different kinds of power. How can we describe Jesus' power?
  The John reading could be read in parts.

Call to Worship

Jesus Christ loves us and has set us free.
He has made of us a royal house to serve as the priests of his God and Father.
To him be the glory and dominion for ever.   **Amen**

Meditation

Lord of lords,
your fate lay in the hands
of an indecisive
Roman official,
looking to cover his own back,
while, albeit unwillingly,
allowing them, the men of brawn,
to scourge yours.

King of kings,
your fate lay in the hands
of a fickle crowd,
manipulated
by frightened politicians.
The avenging Messiah the people acclaimed;
the majesty of suffering love
they mocked.

Judge of judges,
our fate lies in your hands.
We stand before you
in trusting confidence,

for you see – with the eye of love,
hear – with the ear of mercy;
and you sentence
as the one
who himself bears all our suffering.

Prayer of Intercession

Lord of lords, we pray for all those with authority and influence,
asking that they may use their power wisely and well, looking to
the standards of your kingdom of love and justice, peace and
truth.

King of kings, we pray for the leaders of the nations,
    for . . .
L: Lord of lords: R: **Hear the prayers of your people**.

Just Judge, we pray for those struggling to right the
    inequalities and injustices of our world, for . . .
L: Lord of lords: R: **Hear the prayers of your people**.

Eternal Wisdom, we pray for those working at the
    boundaries of knowledge and scientific research, for . . .
L: Lord of lords: R: **Hear the prayers of your people**.

Author of the Universe, we pray for those whose spoken or
    written words influence our ways of thinking, for . . .
L: Lord of lords: R: **Hear the prayers of your people**.

Holy One, we pray for all in positions of leadership
    and responsibility within your church, for . . .
L: Lord of lords: R: **Hear the prayers of your people**.

Almighty and ever-loving God, your kingdom come, your will be
done on earth as it is in heaven.
In the name of Christ, our Righteous Lord.   **Amen**

4th Sunday before Christmas
Advent 1

Isa. 52.1–10
Rom. 11.13–24
John 7.25–31

Presentation

A crown on the communion table, or alongside the Advent wreath will emphasize Jesus as King and the coming Kingdom of God. A second crown, of thorns, would link triumph with suffering.

Call to Worship

'Good News! Your God has become King!'
Raise your voices in song and shout together in joy.
We, who know Christ, come to worship in his name.

Advent Candles

The first candle is lit, and the candle-lighter says:
  This candle is lit to tell us that Christ is
  coming. He brings hope to a troubled world.
  Just as the Israelites needed to be freed from
  Egypt so we need to be set free from our
  worries and fears to live as citizens of God's
  kingdom.

Prayer of Expectation

We wait impatiently for the festival,
  for Christmas with all its joy and happiness.
We wait impatiently for the day,
  for cards, presents and good food.
We wait impatiently for the celebration,
  for decorations, holly and carols.

We wait impatiently for Jesus,
  for the baby of Bethlehem born to be king.
We wait impatiently for the Word,
  for the retelling of the story of salvation.
We wait impatiently for the Christ,
  for the risen Lord, who raises us to new life.
Come, Lord, come quickly.
Fill our hearts, now, with your love and joy.   **Amen**

Prayer *After the congregation have shared their news*

Good News! Jesus, the Son of God, was born in Bethlehem.
He shared our human life, he knew joy and sorrow, he laughed
and cried, he was like us.
God of happiness, we thank you for all the good news we hear
today . . .
(*Births, marriages, visits, anniversaries, etc.*)

Sad News. Jesus, the chosen one of God, was crucified in
Jerusalem. Few recognized him as the true Son of God. Many
thought him a trouble maker, a dangerous man.
God of sorrow, we confess the bad news we hear today . . .
(*Wars, hunger, hatred, things that need to be changed*)

Good News! Jesus rose from the dead and will come again in
glory. He will triumph over evil, he will bring peace to the
nations, he will complete the Kingdom of Heaven here on earth.
God of love, we place in your hands the news which, until then,
brings us pain . . .
(*Mention sick people, those who have died, worries*)

Loving God, we wait for Christmas and await the coming of your
kingdom. Help us to recognize your presence through all the
news we hear and to trust you to fulfil all your promises. **Amen**

Offering Prayer

At this time of year, Lord,
may we never forget the needs of others.
As we offer these gifts,
help us to use our money wisely,
to bring love, joy and peace to others
as well as to buy good things for ourselves. **Amen**

Blessing

As you wait through Advent and prepare to celebrate Christ's
birth, may God bless you and keep you,
fill you with hope, calm you with peace,
and inspire you with love. **Amen**

3rd Sunday before Christmas

Presentation

This is Bible Sunday, so let the Bible 'lead' the worship. The Old Testament reading is difficult for children. Use Psalm 19 in a responsive form instead. Bring the Bible into church with special care, or emphasize its importance when opening it at the day's reading. Use the occasion to remind people how precious the Bible is and to treat it with reverence.

Use the words, 'Look and listen, this is God's Word!'

Call to Worship

We come together to worship God,
    to sing, to pray, to listen to the Bible
    and to learn its message for us today.
May the words of our mouths and the thoughts
    of our minds be acceptable to you,
O Lord, our strength and redeemer.

Advent Candles

One candle should be lit before the service starts.
The second candle is lit. The candle-lighter says:
    This candle is lit for the writers of the Bible,
    and especially for the prophets who told people
    about God and about the right way to live.

Prayer before the Bible Readings

Living God, you inspired the writers of the Bible.
The prophets passed on what they heard you say to them.
The Psalmist wrote great poems and prayers.
L: For your holy word:
R: **Thank you, God**.

The Gospel writers wrote down stories about Jesus and his
teaching. Luke told how the disciples continued Jesus' mission
and ministry. The letter writers shared their faith and knowledge.
L: For your holy word:
R: **Thank you, God**.

L: As we listen to the Bible, help us:
R: **To understand what we hear and to learn its message for our
lives today. Amen**

Meditation

Who tells the truth?
The politician, the estate-agent, the parent?
Who are we to believe?
The weather-forecaster, the teacher, the journalist?

Every day we make judgments,
about what is true and what is false,
what is right and what is wrong.
We live by making decisions based on
what we are told and what we think we know.

This is truth:
   that Jesus is the Son of God.
This we believe:
   that he came to save us.

Lord, help us to assess what we are told
and to recognize your truth.
Help us to live our lives
by what we truly know of you and your love.

Dismissal

In the beauty of the world, see God.
In the word of a neighbour, hear God.
In the touch of a friend, feel God.
In your heart and mind, know God.
In your actions, love God.
Go with God.
God goes with you. **Amen**

2nd Sunday before Christmas
Advent 3

Mal. 4.1–6
I Cor. 4.1–5
John 1.19–28

Presentation

Place the font close to the Advent candles to show that today we remember John who baptized those who repented. Other items such as the Baptism Register and a Baptism candle can be placed alongside.

A candle or candles will be needed for the dismissal.

Call to Worship

A voice cries in the wilderness,
'Make straight the way of the Lord.'
We too prepare for the coming of the Lord, the birth of Jesus,
and make straight our lives to meet our God.

Meditation – Waiting Still

He came, with healing.
He came, with comfort.
He came, with peace.
He came, with love.
Jesus, the kings of kings,
came to be with his people. Prepare to celebrate his birth.

Advent Candles

Two candles should be lit before the service starts.
The third candle is lit and the candle-lighter says:
   This candle is lit for John the Baptist who came to prepare
   hearts and minds for the coming of the Son of God. It shines
   with the light of forgiveness for those who have turned to
   follow Jesus.

Prayer of Confession

L: Still the world is full of evil.
   Still we speak words of hatred.
   Still we do selfish things.
   Still we need to hear John's call to repent.
R: **We are sorry for all our wrong words and deeds and
   ask to be forgiven**.

L: Hear the good news; 'Your sins are forgiven'.
  Through Jesus' birth, his life and death and
  resurrection, we have a new birth, a new start.
R: **Glory to God who comes to save his people**.
L: Hear the word of the Lord: 'Go forth and sin no more.'
R: **Thanks be to God.   Amen**

Prayer of Thanksgiving

Thank you, Creator God,
- for the sun which gives light to the world,
  which is there even when covered with cloud;
- for the light of moon and stars,
  so far away that their brightness seems dim to us.

Thank you, Father God,
- for your Son Jesus, the light of the world, here since
  before time, born in Bethlehem, alive still and for ever,
  even when we do not recognize his presence.

Thank you, Spirit of God,
- for the light you shed on the Bible,
- for preachers and teachers who share the good news
  and interpret it for us, even when our minds
  do not understand.

Thank you, Living God,
- for the light of your gospel which guides our lives.
  You illuminate the truth, you shine with love,
  you are radiant with glory

As we see the lights of Christmas, candles and decorations, may
we know the true light of life burning in us.   **Amen**

Dismissal   *As this is read, a candle can be carried out of
  the church or individual candles lit for the people*

Follow Jesus in all you do.
Take his light into the dark places of the world and show people
what is good and true. Go with God.   **Amen**

Sunday next before Christmas
Advent 4

Call to Worship

If possible have a soloist sing a setting of the Magnificat – 'Tell out my soul . . .' Alternatively, ask a woman to read: Luke 1.46b–48.

Advent Candles

Three candles should be lit before the service starts.
The fourth candle is lit and the candle-lighter says:
This candle is lit for Mary the mother of Jesus. We remember her and Elizabeth, the mother of John, who were happy because they were chosen by God for a special purpose. We give thanks for all mothers and fathers who set a good example to their children and bring them up in the way of truth and faith.

Prayer of Rejoicing

L: Mary was the first to hear that she was to bear God's Son
R: **We rejoice that he is coming**.
L: Elizabeth and Zechariah named their son John, which means 'the Lord is gracious'.
   John prepared for the coming of Jesus:
R: **We rejoice that he is coming**.
L: Soon we shall celebrate Christ's birth at Christmas:
R: **We rejoice that he is coming**.
L: Jesus is with us, we praise and worship him:
R: **We rejoice that he is coming**.
L: Lord, come to us, today and every day.
   Help us to be strong in faith and in all we think
   and do.   **Amen**

Prayer (*For use at any point after Bible readings*)

All round the world Christians are preparing for Christmas.
   Like us, they rejoice in the presence of Jesus in the world.
Lord God, we thank you that your Son came as one of us,
   to reveal your love for all people.

All round the world people hear the good news of Christmas and wonder about its meaning for today.
Lord God, we thank you for all who, like us, want to share the good news.
Help your people everywhere so to present it, in word and deed, that the world may understand and believe.

All round the world Christians rejoice, at Christmas-time, in the presence of Jesus in the church.
Lord God, we thank you for the joy we share at hearing again the stories of Jesus' birth.
Help us, in gratitude, to worship you sincerely now and to serve you faithfully in the year ahead.   **Amen**

Prayer of Intercession

We pray for all parents with the responsibility of caring for their children . . .   (*new parents, baptism families*)
May the example of Mary encourage them in their task.

We pray for all the leaders of the nations with the responsibility of caring for their people . . .   (*countries in the news*)
May they, like Elizabeth, receive understanding through your Spirit.

We pray for all the members of the church, the family of God, with the responsibility of sharing your
good news . . .   (*mention special concerns*)
May Christians everywhere be inspired by the self-sacrifice of Christ who sought only to do his Father's will.

We pray for ourselves, with the responsibility of becoming the
people you want us to be.   *Silence*
May we always find re-assurance in Jesus' promise to be with his disciples to the end of the age.   **Amen**

Christmas Day

Isa. 62.6–7, 10–12
Titus 3.4–7
John 1.1–14 *or* Luke 2.1–20

Presentation

A cracker's contents can demonstrate the message of Christmas;
the cracker – itself the bright colours of the 'secular' Christmas;
the joke – who would have thought that God would come as a baby!
or the motto – the Word of God given to us;
the gift – the gift of forgiveness shown in the cross;
the hat – a crown for the King.
   This can be adapted in many ways, even to constructing a large cracker containing specially made items.

Call to Worship

Jesus, born in Bethlehem, be born in us today,
so that we can share your eternal life.
Jesus the saviour has come!
Glory to God, his Father and ours!

Advent Candles

Four candles are lit before the service starts.
The fifth candle is lit at the very start of worship and the candle-lighter says:
   This candle is lit for the Son of God.
   Lord Christ, baby Jesus, welcome to your world.

Litany of Glory

L: Hear the good news of great joy:
   Jesus, God's Son has come. Glory to God:
R: **And peace to the world**.
L: Jesus, the teacher has come. Glory to God:
R: **And peace to the world**.
L: Jesus, the healer has come. Glory to God:
R: **And peace to the world**.

L: Jesus, the light has come. Glory to God:
R: **And peace to the world**.
L: Jesus, the deliverer has come. Glory to God:
R: **And peace to the world**.
L: Jesus, the friend has come. Glory to God:
R: **And peace to the world**.
L: Sing praise to God. Glory to God:
R: **And peace to the world**.   **Amen**

Prayers of Adoration and Petition

Father God,
you do not think like us and your ways are not our ways.
We can only marvel at all that you have done, for us and for all
people, through the baby born in Bethlehem and the man he
grew up to be.
He brought light to a dark world;
he brings light to our puzzled minds;
he will bring to us the light of heavenly glory.

Forgive us that we often prefer darkness to light.
Help us, when the celebrations of Christmas are over, not to lose
sight of Jesus in the darkness and distractions of our busy lives.
As we follow him, may the light of life illuminate our path of
discipleship.   **Amen**

Offering prayer

Father God,
through the offering of your Son, Jesus, all that was necessary for
the world's salvation was achieved.
May these gifts, and our lives,
be offered in love and used to reveal your love
and to spread the good news of salvation.
Bless them and us in your service.   **Amen**

Final Blessing

Christ's peace surround you,
Christ's light shine upon you,
Christ's joy fill you,
Christ's blessing always go with you.   **Amen**

1st Sunday after Christmas

Presentation

Despite being born in a stable, Jesus came as a king – that is one point of Matthew's story of the visit of the Magi. Despite obvious disharmony the world is meant to live in unity – that is the point of Isaiah's ideal vision.

Both passages relate to messianic deliverance, and Matthew indicates how costly that will be for God. Explain that, against the background of these themes, Christmas can never be simply a time of fun and laughter, for there is a serious message to be learnt. It reminds us of God's surprising way of working – foolishness to many but the true wisdom of God.

Call to Worship

In the Christian family there is no difference
between rich and poor, slave and free, male and female.
All are alike to God, all equally loved by him.
Together we worship as God's sons and daughters
through the Spirit.

Prayer of Thanksgiving

Gold for royalty!
Jesus, you are Lord, and gold was a fitting gift for you.
Born in poverty, you never owned great wealth, never sought
riches, never wanted paying for your labour.
For you were rich in love,
the gift you give to us, beyond our deserving.
L. For all your gifts: R. **We thank you Jesus**.

Frankincense for a God!
Jesus, you are God's chosen one, and for you frankincense was a
fitting gift.
The wise men recognized you as someone destined to change the
world. Yet you were humble and came as a servant.
For you were holiness itself, and through you
we are made holy, beyond our deserving.
L. For all your gifts: R. **We thank you Jesus**.

Myrrh for a burial!
Jesus, even at your birth your death was prophesied, and myrrh
was a fitting gift.
Yet by your death we are made alive.
For your ultimate gift to us was your life, the gift remembered in
bread and wine, beyond our deserving.
L. For all your gifts: R. **We thank you Jesus**.

Gold, frankincense and myrrh, great gifts for Jesus.
Love, holiness and life – great gifts given by Jesus.
L. For all your gifts: R. **We thank you Jesus.   Amen**

Offering Prayer

The wise men worshipped you and brought you gifts.
Accept the gifts we bring, our possessions, our love and our lives,
all given in your service.   **Amen**

Prayer of Hope

Lord, it's easy
    to dismiss the vision of Isaiah as wishful thinking;
    to smile knowingly at the thought of calves and lion
        cubs eating together, and a child taking care of them;
    to forget the other half of the vision, about justice
        and integrity and recognizing the rights of the helpless.
Help us to see that this need not be wishful thinking.
We have spoiled your world by our selfishness, pride and hatred,
yet with your love it can still be transformed.
Help us, by your Spirit,
    to grow in wisdom and understanding;
    to have respect for you and knowledge of your ways;
May your kingdom come with justice and peace, so that the
vision may be fulfilled.   **Amen**

Dismissal

With the freedom which the Spirit gives,
go and live as God's sons and daughters
in the service of Jesus Christ, our Lord and Saviour.   **Amen**

2nd Sunday after Christmas

Presentation

A theme in each of the readings this week is growth: growth of the individual in wisdom and faith, and growth of the church. This could be presented in a variety of ways – introduce a number of people of different ages who have grown in height or in knowledge; explain how the church still needs to grow; illustrate the development in understanding of Christ and his will for us. Ask one or more people to talk about their own growing faith.

Call to Worship

No one has seen God,
but as we get to know Jesus we come close to the Father.
Jesus, God's Son, was born a human being, made his home in
this world and showed us God in his grace and truth.
Let us then worship God the Father as we see him in Jesus.

Prayer of Thanksgiving

God, Father of our Lord Jesus Christ,
We thank you that, in your love,
   you have created the world and revealed yourself in it.
We thank you that, in your love,
   you have helped us to understand your gospel and to
   know Jesus as our friend.
We thank you that, in your love,
   you have brought us to faith and filled our hearts with
   love for others.
Help us, day by day, to grow in faith, love and
   understanding and, by the strength which your Spirit
   gives, to be confirmed in your service.
May we never grow weary on our Christian journey but have the
energy of eagles on soaring wings.
May we, with all your church, reveal your glory, in our
community and wherever in the world we go.   **Amen**

Offering Prayer

We offer our gifts, praying that, through this church and the
mission of the church world-wide, God's glory may be revealed.
May the grace of God sustain all his work for his
kingdom. **Amen**

Meditation – Imagine Growth

Shut your eyes, concentrate, and picture what I say.

Imagine a tiny seed, planted in good soil.
Warmth and moisture stimulate its growth.
A root appears, and then a tiny shoot,
at first no bigger than a pinhead, aiming for the light.
All of a sudden the shoot breaks through the surface and is
flooded in light.
It grows more quickly, two leaves appear, the shoot climbs,
white growth turns green in the sunlight;
more leaves sprout from below.
A bud, crowning the fully grown plant,
bursts open, revealing a glorious flower.
Scent fills the air and bees take their fill of the nectar.
When the flower dies,
fallen petals lay a carpet of colour on the damp earth.
And seeds, dropping into the rich soil,
find all that is necessary for growth to begin again.

Let us pray:
Lord, take the seed of our faith, water it with your grace, warm it
with your love; and as it grows in the light of your word, help us
to reflect your glory to the world,
and to fill the world with the sweetness of your kindness and
compassion.
So may the seed of faith be planted in others and nurtured by
your grace and love. **Amen**

Blessing

May grace and truth grow in you,
may light and strength flow from you,
may love and hope be showered upon you,
and may God's blessing be with you, evermore. **Amen**

1st Sunday after Epiphany

Isa. 42.1–9
Eph. 2.1–10
John 1.29–34

Presentation

Who is this Jesus, whose birth we have celebrated? Today looks forward to the stories about Jesus as teacher, healer, bringer of justice, forgiver, saviour, etc.

Using a large 'body' put different words on the parts – hand for healing touch, foot for traveller, heart for love, etc. as a focus for thinking about Jesus' tasks.

Call to Worship

Jesus is the chosen one. He sheds light on our path,
brings justice and hope, and takes away the sin of the world.
We, his followers, worship in his name.

Prayer of Confession

It is easy to take the way of the world,
    to think only of ourselves,
    to be greedy, dishonest
    and eager to possess what rightly belongs to others.

It is hard to acknowledge that we can do nothing, in the
    end, to save ourselves from the harm which such
    attitudes do to others and ourselves.

Yet we want to have the assurance that we are loved by
    God and will be united with him in heaven.
And God's promises are sure,
    the way of salvation has been opened for us.

Lord God, we thank you
    that we can share life with Christ,
    on earth and in heaven,
    that through your grace we are forgiven
    and through Jesus we can be saved.

It is easy to hear your words: 'Your sins are forgiven.'
It is hard to receive them for ourselves.
Saviour, help us to accept your mercy and understand your

endless love. Strengthen our faith and fill us with your Holy
Spirit, in Jesus' name.   **Amen**

Meditation

'God's chosen one'.
What a calling! What a challenge!
How did you feel, Jesus, when you were baptized?
How did you feel when so many expected so much from you?
Daunted, unworthy, proud, frightened?

You set about your task with courage,
a courage in your relationship with your Father.
You felt secure in his love, sure that he was guiding your
footsteps and would never fail you.

What about me?
Through you, Lord Jesus, I too am 'chosen of God'.
What a calling, what a challenge!
I feel daunted, I feel unworthy,
I feel afraid, and a little proud.
So much is expected of me,
for you now look to me to be your mouth, your ears, your hands,
your feet in the world today.

May I set about my task with courage,
a courage rooted in my relationship with you.
Help me to feel secure in your love,
sure that you are guiding my life
and will never fail me.

'There goes the Lamb of God', said John the Baptist.
What will people say about me?
'There *he* (*she*) goes to church?
There goes a friend of Jesus?
There goes a good *man* (*woman*) ?
There goes a believer in God?
Help me, guide me, show me,
how to live up to my calling,
the challenge of being a 'chosen one of God'.

2nd Sunday after Epiphany

Presentation

*An exercise in listening – identifying sounds on a tape, famous voices,
chinese whispers – will get the congregation thinking about listening
to God. The John reading could be effectively mimed by 'calling'
people out of the congregation.*

Call to Worship   *Adapt to your situation*

Come, factory worker, clerk, shop assistant, teacher.
Come, manager, nurse, council worker, pupil.
Come, parent, child, visitor, friend.
Come, hear the call of Jesus to you,
Come, worship as Christ's disciples.

Prayer of Adoration

We praise you, wonderful God,
for revealing yourself to your creation.
You did not leave us in the dark about you:
   your light has illuminated your nature,
   just as the sun illuminates your world.
We praise you, almighty God,
   for revealing yourself to your people.
   You spoke through the prophets,
   and even if people did not heed your words,
   you continued to encourage and guide them.
We praise you, Father God,
   for revealing yourself through your son, Jesus.
   Through his words and deeds, he showed your finest
   virtues – mercy, peace and love – and astonished all
   who saw them.
We praise you, wise God,
   for revealing yourself through the Holy Spirit.
   She inspires us, brings us close to you
   and binds us to you in love.
We praise you, God of all time and every place,
   for revealing yourself to us, so that we can know you.   **Amen**

Prayer of Listening   *Tell the congregation there will be*
   silences for listening to God speaking to us

What have you to say to the world, God of justice?
We speak to you of hunger, of war, of corruption,
of refugees, of suspicion and hatred.
We pray for wisdom to show the world a better way.
Silence
L: Lord, this is our prayer:
R: **Help us to know and do your will**.

What have you to say to the church, God of faith?
We speak to you of plans and visions,
of doubts and mistrust, of hopes and fears.
We pray for guidance to be your servants to the community.
Silence
L: Lord, this is our prayer:
R: **Help us to know and do your will**.

What have you to say to those who suffer, God of love?
We speak to you of friends, neighbours and strangers who, sick
in body, mind or spirit, are in need of care.
We pray for healing and wholeness for them.
Silence
L: Lord, this is our prayer:
R: **Help us to know and do your will**.

What have you to say to us, God of all?
We speak to you of our longings, of difficult choices,
of divided loyalties and of wonderful opportunities.
We pray for faith to follow the movement of your Spirit.
Silence
L: Lord, this is our prayer:
R: **Help us to know and do your will**.

God who has spoken throughout history,
help us to hear your voice calling to us today.   **Amen**

3rd Sunday after Epiphany

Presentation

*How do we recognize God? Moses wasn't allowed to see God's face
but John asserts that 'we have seen [the Word of life] with our own
eyes.' Jesus reveals his nature by his first sign and miracle at Cana.*

*Use photographs to illustrate the problem of identifying people or
objects from strange angles.*

Use I John 1 at the very start of worship.

Call to Worship

Join in fellowship with the Father and his Son Jesus Christ so that
you may have life, eternal life, which has existed from the
beginning and will last to the end.

Prayer of Thanksgiving

It overflowed,
– wine in abundance, gallons and gallons of it.
  You didn't just give enough to drink,
  you didn't just give ordinary wine.
  It was the best and more than enough for everyone.

It overflows,
– love in abundance, hugs and hugs of it.
  You don't just give enough to suffice,
  you don't just give ordinary love.
  It is the best and more than enough for everyone.

Loving Lord, we thank you for your abundant love:
– love which lets us know we are not alone;
– love which comforts our pain and suffering;
– love which embraces our joy;
– love which changes our lives
  and blesses us with life eternal.

Loving Lord, may we share abundant love:
– love for our family;
– love for our friends;

- love for the stranger, and even for our enemy;
- love to give comfort;
- and love which overflows without thought for ourselves.

Thank you, Lord, for your example of selfless giving.
May we follow you and be able to show others
the sign of your presence in the world. **Amen**

Prayer of Intercession

'That is no concern of mine'.
How quickly it comes to our lips, how easy to wash our hands of
problems and continue in our own sweet way.

But, Lord, you answered the bridegroom's need,
doing what was necessary to save his face.

Lord, answer the needs of the world, doing what is necessary to
bring peace, justice and eternal life for all.
The world is your concern and ought to be ours,
and we look to you to help us bring change.

Where there is hatred:	**Strengthen us to pour your love**.
Where there is hunger:	**Guide us to fill the food-stores**.
Where there is illness:	**Inspire us to bring health**.
Where there is loneliness:	**Help us to spread fellowship**.
Where there is war:	**Challenge us to show your peace**.

Change attitudes, change lives, change us.
May your concerns become our concerns,
may your ways be our ways,
and may our love reveal your glory. **Amen**

Final Words and Blessing

As Jesus changed water into wine at Cana as a sign of his coming
glory, may he change us from sinners to lovers as a sign of his
glory in the world today.
God bless you with all you need for life.
Go in love and live your lives for his glory. **Amen**

4th Sunday after Epiphany

I Kings 8.22–30
I Cor. 3.10–17
John 2.13–25

Presentation

*Although we cannot contain the divine presence, we worship God in
the Temple – which can be the world itself, or the sanctuary, or
Christ's body, the holy people of God. Ask the congregation where
they experience the presence of God, and incorporate their answers
into an opening prayer of adoration and praise.*

Call to Worship

There is no God like the Lord our God,
in heaven above or on earth beneath,
constant in love to those who faithfully serve.
Let us worship the Lord in his Temple.

Prayer of Confession   *After Old Testament reading*

God of sustaining love,
  you are our God,
  we are your people.
You have given us this world
  in which to live and grow,
  in which to know and praise you,
  in which to respond to your love.

We confess that our lives are poor in worship.
We do not look for your presence in our everyday lives.
L: Holy and loving God, hear us in heaven your dwelling:
R: **And when you hear, forgive**.

We confess that our lives are poor in worship.
We bring distracted, half-hearted selves
  to times of prayer and praise.
L: Holy and loving God, hear us in heaven your dwelling:
R: **And when you hear, forgive**.

We confess that our lives are poor in worship.
We shy away from sharing our faith with those we know.
L: Holy and loving God, hear us in heaven your dwelling:
R: **And when you hear, forgive**.

We confess that our lives are poor in worship.
We grasp at your love but find it hard to be loving
   to you or to others.
L: Holy and loving God, hear us in heaven your dwelling:
R: **And when you hear, forgive**.

We make our prayers through Jesus Christ,
   whose body was a temple torn down and built again,
   that we might be forgiven.   **Amen**

Prayers of Intercession

The world is God's temple. Let us pray for the world:
– for the powerful, that they may know that the world
   belongs not to them but to the God of love and justice;
– for the powerless, that they may know that God is
   alongside them in their hunger, fear and suffering.
Silence

The church is God's temple. Let us pray for the church:
– for its leaders, that they may guide their people and
   the world to worship in word and deed;
– for the different denominations, that in unity they may
   come to know and worship the one, undivided God.
Silence

We are God's temple. Let us pray for ourselves:
– for this congregation, that we may become a sanctuary
   for the lonely, the worried and the sad, a people of
   love and hope;
– for each one of us, that our lives may be hymns of
   worship to the eternal God, sung in confidence and joy.
Silence

In the name of our High Priest, Jesus Christ.   **Amen**

Dismissal

Hear the words of the apostle:
   'You are God's building.
    The temple of God is holy and you are that temple.'
Go, live and love to his praise and glory.   **Amen**

5th Sunday after Epiphany

Presentation

*God's word of truth can come to us in many ways and our reponse to
it is the most crucial judgment we ever make. Parables, symbols and
Christ himself draw out life-altering responses from us. After
explaining the context, act out the Judges reading and ask the
congregation for their understanding of it and what it says to us
today.*

Call to Worship

Come in wonder to adore the God of mystery.
Come in trust to praise the God of love.
Let all the world worship
the God of truth and grace.

Prayer of Praise

Lord, we are a small people,
   small in mind and short on understanding,
   limited in vision,
   living careful, finite lives.
You are a great God,
   whose mind knows, sees and understands
   all that is
   and you love immensely and for ever.

Lord, how can we offer you the worship of praise
   with our small, weak voices?
How can we offer you the worship of our lives
   which are so powerless and short?
How can we offer you the worship of our love
   which is so shallow and limited?

Lord, yours is the greatness that fills creation.
Yet the immensity of your love
   came to us in a new-born child.
You speak to us in stories, pictures, signs,
   that we may grasp at truths too great for our minds.

Lord, we praise you, for in your generosity
you accept in love the poorest of our offerings.
Take our little lives, and make them great in you.   **Amen**

Prayers of Intercession

Let us pray for all seekers after truth:

For the leaders of the nations,
   who seek right ways to govern their people:
L: God of wisdom, your word is truth:
R: **Open our ears to your voice**.

For the electors of governments,
   who seek to use their votes to benefit others:
L: God of wisdom, your word is truth:
R: **Open our ears to your voice**.

For all who explore what it means to be human,
   through writing, music, art and dance,
   seeking to give us understanding of ourselves:
L: God of wisdom, your word is truth:
R: **Open our ears to your voice**.

For those confused and disorientated by illness,
   grief or sorrow, who seek the way ahead:
L: God of wisdom, your word is truth:
R: **Open our ears to your voice**.

For all on the journey of faith, who seek reassurance:
L: God of wisdom, your word is truth:
R: **Open our ears to your voice**.

In the name of Jesus Christ,
   your word of salvation to us.   **Amen**

Dismissal

God is waiting for you in the world,
waiting to speak to you in all you see and hear.
Go, and live the way of love and truth,
guided by God's voice within you.   **Amen**

YEAR D

YEAR D

6th Sunday after Epiphany

Deut. 5.12–15
II Cor. 2.14–3.6
John 7.14–24

Presentation

It is very easy to go by appearances and to put more emphasis on the externals of faith than on our relationship with God. Ask an older member of the congregation to describe how Sunday was kept sixty years ago. Then ask the congregation to make a list of 'do's and don'ts' for Sunday today, with faith reasons for them. Turn this list into a prayer, with the versicle and response:
L: Loving God, you have made Sunday for us:
R: **Help us to know and to show your love today**.

Call to Worship

On Sunday Christ came back from the dead.
This is a special, holy day.
Let us offer God our hearts and souls and minds
in loving praise and prayer.

Prayer of Confession

All-seeing God,
you do not judge by appearances.
You see straight to the heart of us.
You know what is there and yet you love us.
We can come to you in openness and trust.

All-knowing God,
we want to offer you our worship on this holy day,
for you are our God.
We respect you. We love you. We rely upon you.

All-loving God,
we confess the poverty of that worship,
for we are poor in love, our will to do good is weak,
we lack concentration
when it comes to your kingdom.

All-merciful God,
we can never be worthy of you,
yet you still love us and delight in our worship.

160

Help us to worship you with the whole of our lives,
that we may truly become a people for your praise.

Meditation *Could use a separate questioner*

Are you a follower of Jesus?
Yes, I'm a Christian.
I go to church.
I do my bit for charity.
I try to be nice.

Are you a follower of Jesus?
Yes, I'm a Christian.
I wear cheerful but challenging badges.
I quote the Bible.
I try to be friendly.

Are you a follower of Jesus?
Yes, I'm a Christian.
I do a lot for the church.
I write for the newsletter.
I try to be helpful.

But are you a follower of Jesus?
Yes, I'm a Christian,
for I love.
Even when the going is rough
and my heart is afraid,
my mind full of doubt,
I still, painfully, love.
Yes, I follow Jesus.

Blessing

May the laws of God be written on your hearts
and the love of God be written in your lives.
May the blessing of God, Creator, Redeemer, Sustainer,
be with you now and evermore.   **Amen**

9th Sunday before Easter

Presentation

Claiming to know the truth, as revealed to us in the gospel, can sometimes have the effect of making us arrogant or intolerant. The readings this Sunday show that our knowledge of the truth bears fruit in our lives, in right living (Job), love (II John) and freedom (John).

Make a number of statements about things, animals, people etc. (e.g. dogs have four legs) and ask the congregation whether they are true and how they know. Finish with the statement, 'God is love.'

Call to Worship

Let us be true worshippers of the ever-living God.
Let us worship in spirit and in truth

Prayer of Adoration

Creator God,
    yours is the mind behind all that is,
    yours is the Wisdom that rules creation.
    You know all that there is to know.
    You see all that there is to see.
    You are all truth.

Saviour God,
    yours is the loving mind revealed in Jesus Christ,
    yours is the wise Word made flesh.
    You have made yourself a God we can know.
    You have given us a glimpse of yourself, of your
    eternal truth.

Uniting God,
    yours is the Spirit that brings understanding,
    yours is the Spirit that makes us wise.
    You change our lives as we come to know you.
    You give us new ways of seeing the world, new truths
    to set us free,
God of all truth – we worship you.

Prayer of Confession

Lord, we have not listened to your truth.
We have not let your truth set us free.

We have claimed to know the truth,
   and claimed to be better than others,
   the sinful and ignorant and damned.
We have claimed to know the truth,
   but we have not really listened,
   and we are not set free.

We have claimed to know the truth,
   and claimed to be wiser than others,
   the seekers, the questioners, the doubters.
We have claimed to know the truth,
   but we have not really listened,
   and we are not set free.

Lord, forgive us.
Open our ears
   to listen to your truth.
Open our hearts
   that we may live by your truth.
We pray that your truth will make us
   loving and humble,
   seekers after understanding,
   keen to do what is right.
We pray that your truth may set us free
   from all that keeps us from you.

In the Name of Jesus Christ,
the Way, the Truth and the Life.   **Amen**

Dismissal

You have been entrusted with the gospel of Christ.
Go and proclaim it to the world:
the truth for living
and the truth for giving.

8th Sunday before Easter

Presentation

Our faith in a loving God may be tested when life gets difficult but our lessons today remind us that such testing need not be a cause for despair. Though we may feel we cannot find God, God has not turned his face against us (Job). We can ask for strength to overcome all that cripples our lives (John). And endurance through the testing of our faith makes better Christians of us (James).

The Job reading could be done effectively by two voices. Allow time for silent meditation after the short passage from James. This passage could also be linked with a biographical reading or a testimony.

Call to Worship

Come all who wish to worship the Lord,
Come and praise the God of our salvation.
Come, all you faithful, come, all with doubts,
Come, all you who seek the Lord,
Come, and praise the God of our salvation.

Prayer of Intercession

Lord, it is hard, when we look at the created world,
　　to have faith in you as the God of love. We see floods
　　and earthquakes, drought and famine, accident and disease,
　　and we long for you to make your creation perfect.

Yet you, God of creation, are the God we know in Christ,
　　who healed the sick, fed the hungry, comforted the sad.

And so Lord, in faith we pray to you,
　　for those who are suffering in any way, for . . .
L: The Lord hears our prayer:
R: **Thanks be to God**.

Lord, it is hard, when we look at humankind, to have faith
in you as the God of love. We see hatred and warfare,
violence and abuse, injustice and oppression, and we long
for your justice and the end of the power of evil.

Yet you, God of humankind, are the God we know in Christ,
a man who loved to the uttermost, even to death on the
cross.

And so Lord, in faith we pray to you, for those who are
the victims of the inhumanity of others, for . . .
L: The Lord hears our prayer:
R: **Thanks be to God**.

Lord, there can be many times, on our journey through life,
when we find it hard to have faith in you as the God of
love. We see the failures of the church to live up to
its calling as Christ's body in the world. People we love
are taken from us. Good people suffer bad things.
We long for the coming of your kingdom of peace and joy.

Yet you, the God of life, are the God we know in Christ,
who came to be our friend and Saviour, to lead us from
darkness into light and eternal life.

And so Lord, in faith we pray to you,
for ourselves and for your church,
that we may endure times of testing, for . . .
L: The Lord hears our prayer:
R: **Thanks be to God**.

In the name of Christ our Lord, who endured to the end and was
raised again to glory.   **Amen**

Dismissal

You have not been promised an easy life.
You have not been promised a safe life.
But you have been promised real, eternal life.
Go out and live that life in Christ.

7th Sunday before Easter

Presentation

In all three passages we find the Word of God providing for both the spiritual and physical needs of humankind. We too must care not for the body or soul alone but for the whole person. This is a good Sunday to explore issues of world hunger (rather than in the Harvest Thanksgiving). The John reading could be dramatized.

Prepare a display of 'bare necessities': bread, water, clothing, medicine, Bible, photo of church group etc., to be used as a basis for thanksgiving or intercessory prayers.

Opening Sentences

We cannot live on bread alone.
We live on every word that comes
from the mouth of the Lord.

Prayer of Adoration and Confession

Creating God,
>   we marvel at the beauty and order of your world;
>   at the variety and uniqueness of creatures and plants,
>   and that each has its own place in nature's plan.

Creating God,
>   we marvel at the provision that you have made
>   for your special creation, humankind.
>   We praise you for your many gifts to us
>   and that we can know you as our Mother and Father God.

Creating God,
>   We confess that we have not looked after your world.
>   We have exploited its resources and its peoples.
>   Our greed has led to pollution, hunger and injustice.

Forgive us, we pray,
>   and restore us to our proper place in your plan.
Teach us the right way to live in your world
>   as followers of the Saviour Lord.   **Amen**

Meditation

He was hungry, yet he laughed.
She was well-fed, yet she cried.

Lord, there are so many different kinds of hunger
in this starving world of ours.
There are so many crying out to be fed.

We can hardly bear to see
the starving children on our television screens,
with their fleshless limbs, huge, soulful eyes,
absurdly swollen stomachs.
Yet might not those images of malnourished bodies
also be pictures of the souls of the well-fed?
Of souls crying out for spiritual food?
Souls shrivelled up from lack of meaning in their lives.
Souls yearning and searching for love and belonging.
Souls absurdly swollen with empty pride and false
priorities.
Lord, we are surrounded by the starving.
Fill us with your Holy Spirit,
that out of our riches
we may give to those in need
and so continue, in you
the work of Christ in the world.

Offering

Blessed is the Lord our God
who has given us food for our tables
and food for our souls.
Lord God, accept our gifts of thanksgiving
and with them, our lives themselves,
and use us as manna for your world.

Dismissal

Through the power of God, our offering of worship
is transformed into food for the world.
Go out with joy to feed hungry mouths and lives.

6th Sunday before Easter
Lent 1

Presentation

The temptations can be presented in several ways: e.g. by dramatization or by displaying things that tempt us today – not the trivial things such as refraining from sweets, but the greater extravagances of modern society!

During Lent place different objects on a display, culminating in a cross and empty tomb at Easter. Today use stones and bread to represent the temptations.

Call to Worship   (*Heb. 4.16*)

'Let us boldly approach the throne of grace in order that we may receive mercy and find grace to give us timely help.'

Prayer of Approach

'Scripture says, "You shall do homage to the Lord your God and worship him alone." '
God our Father, we come to praise and adore you;
Jesus, our Saviour, we come to honour and thank you;
Holy Spirit, our Enabler, we come to open our very selves to you so that we may worship and serve you as we should.

Prayer of Confession

God, our Judge, all too often
   we have wandered away like lost sheep;
   we have fallen to the temptations of this world;
   we have taken our own wilful way –
      wanting to do the impossible,
      wanting to be the centre of attention,
      wanting to rule the world.

Forgive us, we pray, and help us to rely on the resources you provide, so that, when faced by temptation, we can be victorious by the power of your Spirit.
We ask it in Jesus' name.   **Amen**

Prayer of Intercession   *A framework for topical examples*
God of righteousness and truth,
we bring our prayers for all who today succumb to powerful
temptations and ignore your way:
− for those who have opportunities to help others
  but fail to take them;
− for those who court the limelight out of vanity;
− for those who are given the authority to rule
  and abuse it;
− for those who are self-centred and greedy for power.

May they, and all in need, know the strength and comfort of
Jesus who, having resisted temptation, used all his powers to
bring health and wholeness to the world.   **Amen**

Prayer of Dedication

We dedicate ourselves to you, Lord, praying that our Christian
commitment may be realistic
− about the pressures of evil upon us,
− about the weaknesses in our own nature,
− and about the power of your love.
Help us always to fix our hearts and minds on the values of your
kingdom and not to be enticed by temptations to follow the easy
path.
Accept us, we ask, as we are, and make us the people you want
us to be. For Christ's sake.   **Amen**

Dismissal

May we never look for the easy way through difficulties,
   but always face them with God's help.
May we never resort to self-display,
   but always live humbly before the Lord.
May we never seek personal power,
   but always acknowledge the sovereignty of God.

Let us go forth in peace and in the power of the Spirit, following
the example of Jesus and confident in God's mercy and
love.   **Amen**

5th Sunday before Easter
Lent 2

Presentation

Blindness and sight, metaphorically as much as literally, are linking themes in the readings. The John passage is quite long and could well be told like a story (or even dramatized). Poems about blindness or seeing would complement the readings. Images of light and darkness illustrate the theme in Ephesians. Use aids to sight as a focus for worship – magnifying glass, microscope, spectacles etc.

Call to Worship   (*Eph. 5.8–9*)

'Though once you were in darkness, now as Christians you are light. Prove yourselves at home with light, for where light is there is a harvest of goodness, righteousness and truth.'

Prayer of Confession

Jesus, our Healer, we are blind;
blind to the plight of those who need our help:
   we shut our eyes to the suffering
     of the hungry and homeless;
   we close our minds to the isolation
     of the lonely and unloved;
   we harden our hearts to the pain
     of the poor, on our doorstep and across the world.

Jesus, our Healer, take from us the blindness which afflicts us:
   open our eyes to see
     all that you reveal of your Father's love;
   open our minds to perceive
     the ways we can selflessly give to others;
   open our hearts to know
     the joys which fellowship can bring.

Forgive us, Lord, that we neither see nor accept
   what is staring us in the face.
Enable us to acknowledge the darkness of our lives
   so that we may receive the light of your truth.   **Amen**

Prayer of Thanksgiving

See God has revealed himself in the world.
The God of Israel
    kept the chosen nation safe, even from mighty enemies.
The Son of Man
    performed miracles of healing and gave sight to the
    blind.
The Holy Spirit
    filled the first Christians with the courage to witness
    to the gospel.

Gracious God, we thank you for not leaving your people in
darkness but leading us into the light of your glory.
You have opened our eyes to your goodness,
                opened our ears to your truth,
                opened our hearts to your love.
Help us to open our lips to declare your gospel.   **Amen**

Offering Prayer

We do not have to sit and beg,
we do not have to seek alms in order to live.
Lord, we offer our gifts in thankfulness for all that you have
generously given, asking that through this church and the church
throughout the world others may come to know you as their
Saviour.   **Amen**

Dismissal

If we walk in the light,
with Jesus the Light of the World,
then Christ will shine upon us
and others will see his love in ours.
May the Lord lead us from darkness to light,
                    from evil to goodness,
                    from death to life.
Go in faith,
your faith has enabled you to see the Son of God.

4th Sunday before Easter
Lent 3

Presentation

*In slightly different ways each reading picks up the theme of loyalty
and faith. Whom do we follow and what tempts us to stray from that
path? Ask the congregation for examples of loyalty – football fans,
royalists, families, dogs to their owners! Peter's words in John 6.68
are worthy of consideration: he doesn't know who else can tell him
what true life is, so he chooses to stay with Jesus. The Gospel warns of
betrayal. Add a bag of silver coins to the display leading up to Easter.*

Responsive Call to Worship

Voice 1:   Will you forsake God and serve others?
Voice 2:   No, we shall serve the Lord.
People: **He is our God**.
Voice 1:   Will you do wrong and turn against God?
Voice 2:   No, we shall serve the Lord.
People: **He is our God**.
Voice 1:   Have you chosen God and will you serve him alone?
Voice 2:   Yes, we shall serve the Lord.
People: **He is our God**.

Prayer of Confession

The challenge to follow Jesus,
   to seek only to do your will, Father God,
   to stick to the right path, is always with us.
And we easily stray,
   taking what seems the more attractive road.
We are side-tracked by the example of so-called friends,
                by the pull of fame and fortune,
                by the attractions of the easy life.
Rather than face difficult choices,
   we look for simple options.
Rather than wrestle with the Bible,
   we look for simple answers.
And yet, like Peter,
   we know that the words of Jesus have the ring of truth.

Help us, we pray, willingly to receive them, and with them to
receive the Holy Spirit. So that we may not be led into
temptation but delivered from evil.
In the name of Jesus Christ.   **Amen**

Prayer of Thanksgiving

We remember with thanksgiving
   the great leaders of the Jews, who helped
   'no people' to become 'God's people',
   slaves to become free,
   worshippers of many gods to become followers of the one
   true God.
L: We thank you for your loyal servants:
R: **And seek to follow their example of faith**.

We remember with thanksgiving
   the eleven disciples who faithfully followed Jesus,
   struggled to understand what they saw and heard
   and rejoiced to be preachers of the good news.
L: We thank you for your loyal servants:
R: **And seek to follow their example of faith**.

We remember with thanksgiving
   the first Christians, who took up the message,
   learned to be 'one in Christ', and faced persecution
   in the strength of their new found hope.
L: We thank you for your loyal servants:
R: **And seek to follow their example of faith**.

We remember with thanksgiving
   those who, by their teaching and selfless service, revealed
   to us the love of God and brought us into the church.
L: We thank you for your loyal servants:
R: **And seek to follow their example of faith**.

Accept us, Father God, and by the power of your Spirit,
transform our inadequate faith and faltering loyalty, so that we
may serve you faithfully in this needy world.   **Amen**

I Sam. 9.27–10.1, 6–7
II Cor. 1.15–22
John 12.1–8

3rd Sunday before Easter
Lent 4 (Also see Mothering Sunday)

Presentation

Today the church is still criticized for spending money on buildings,
robes and decorations, instead of giving to the poor. We should
certainly give to charity, but we should also give only the best for
God. A role play between 'Mary' and 'Judas' could tease out these
issues. The Samuel reading reminds us of God's gracious gift to us –
the Holy Spirit – far more valuable than any gift we can give in return.
What we can offer is nothing compared to what we have received.
'Aromatherapy' might stimulate some ideas about the theme. Add
incense or another valuable artefact of worship (chalice, cross, etc.)
to the Lenten display. If you choose the Corinthians reading use the
'Yes – No interlude' from the TV gameshow to introduce it (when
questions must not be answered with 'Yes' or 'No').

Call to Worship (*II Cor. 1.22*)

'God has set his seal upon us and, as a pledge of what is to come,
has given the Spirit to dwell in our hearts.'
Let us worship God,
  with thanks for what has been and what is to come.

Prayer of Adoration

Use this verse as a sung response between each section
Jesus, we adore you,
lay our lives before you, how we love you.

Jesus, if you were here in the flesh we would kneel at your feet.
Receive our worship and adoration in prayer and song,
as we recognize your risen presence with us:

We praise you for revealing the Kingdom of God to us
in word and action, and for your teaching in parable and
commandment, which guide our lives each day:

We praise you for your loving kindness, and for your healing of
broken bodies and damaged minds. You fill us with comfort and
hope as we face difficult or distressing times in life:

We praise you for making known to us God's forgiveness in your death on the cross and glorious resurrection. We come before you humbly, asking to be forgiven for our sins:

As we offer our worship, we offer ourselves to be your faithful followers and servants.   **Amen**

Offering Prayer

With fine oil Mary showed her devotion to you, Lord.
She could not speak of her love for you but expressed it in the best way she knew.
These gifts of money, offered gladly and gratefully,
express our love and desire to serve you.   **Amen**

Prayer of Thanksgiving

The gifts of the Spirit, sweeter than fine perfume,
enrich our lives;
– their fragrance overpowers our senses,
– their worth overwhelms our minds,
– their all-pervading scent breathes peace,
– their persistence gives us hope,
– their vitality fills us with life.
Generous God, we thank you for all the good things with which you shower our lives. May we use them to bring comfort and blessing to all whom we meet.   **Amen**

Dismissal (*II Cor. 1.20*)

You have shown your love for Jesus in worship.
Go now and show his love to your neighbours.
Make your whole lives a sacrifice of praise and adoration.
Let your words and actions say 'Yes' to the Christ who has said God's 'Yes' to you. Give glory to God and through Jesus be bold to say 'Amen', today and for ever.   **Amen**

YEAR D

Mothering Sunday

(Also see 3rd Sunday before Easter)

I Sam. 1.9–20
Heb. 11.1–2, 11–12
Luke 2.41–52

Presentation

The readings remind us that motherhood is not always possible, nor is it always easy. Some women struggle and never know the gift of a child, others struggle with the task of bringing up their child. Be careful to make this, not a day of sentimental joy, but an opportunity to encourage parents to think (and pray) about parenting. The gospel could open up a discussion about a parent's rôle.

Call to Worship

We are in our Father's house,
    meeting to worship him and to share our faith.
    May we grow in wisdom and in favour with God.

Prayer for Motherhood   *Use different voices*

'I thought that motherhood would be wonderful –
pink roly-poly babies smelling of talc –
and I love my children very much. But the dirty
nappies and the broken nights leave me
exhausted and sometimes tired with life.'
Let us pray for tired mothers:
Loving God, too often we are unprepared for the realities of life
and feel shocked or offended by them. We pray for those who
are oppressed by the hard work of caring for their families, that
through the support of spouse, friends and the community they
may find the energy to enjoy their children and treasure a love of
life.

'I never had much love in my childhood so I had
this baby to love and need me. But all she
does is cry and complain, take and take – and I
have no more to give.'
Let us pray for mothers crying out for love:
Loving God, we pray for those who have had an unhappy
upbringing and now have children of their own. May they find
resources to overcome the cycle of lovelessness. May they see

their children as persons in their own right and not use them to
hit back at the hurts and failures in their own lives.

'I thought I would find fulfilment through
bringing up children of my own. But instead I
feel less of a person, bored with housework and
children's talk.'

Let us pray for bored mothers:
Loving God, so many women feel imprisoned in their homes,
shackled with children, mindlessly repeating the same tasks and
answering the same questions. May they find more motivation
and excitement in their lives and the opportunity to find company
and seek fulfilment.

'I thought the baby would bring us together,
give our marriage a shot of love. But she's
another source of resentment and irritation,
feelings that I am too tired to overcome.'

Let us pray for mothers whose marriages are under strain:
Loving God, so often the crying of a child brings new tensions
into a family. Husband and wife find it difficult to adjust to their
new roles and to give one another the love they need. We pray
for new parents that they may not neglect one another or shirk
their responsibilities, but together find joy in the child of their
creating.

Loving God, together we pray and work, as Jesus taught us, for
the transformation of all human life. Help us to provide support
for families and parents, so that we may all grow together in
love.   **Amen**

Offering Prayer

Caring God, like a mother to us all,
   for all your gifts to us,
   especially today for the gifts of life and love,
   we give our grateful thanks.
May these offerings of money be used to share your love
   and bring new life to all your children.   **Amen**

Words of Dismissal

Go in peace,
   and may God grant you what you seek from him.

YEAR D

2nd Sunday before Easter

Lent 5 Passion Sunday

Isa. 63.1–9
Col. 2.8–15
John 12.20–36

Presentation

Plant some seeds (preferably a variety which will sprout during the next fortnight) and use the parable of the dying wheat giving a great harvest (John 12.24) to prepare the way for the next two weeks' exploration of Jesus crucified and risen. Link this to the imagery that our old selves (ways of life) need to die, in order to be raised to new life in Jesus (Col. 2.12 – baptism). The planted seeds can be added to the growing visual display.

Call to Worship

Read John 12. 20–23
In this hour of worship may we meet Jesus
and glorify his name.

Prayer of Confession

Lord, you call us to serve you,
    but too often we look after ourselves first.
You call us to love as you love,
    but we love ourselves and not our neighbours.
You call us to glorify you,
    but we seek glory only for ourselves.

Loving Lord, you were obedient,
    even when obedience led you to the cross.
Fill us, we pray, with your love and enable us to be
    obedient to our calling.
Strip away our selfishness and pride,
    and open our hearts to your forgiveness.
So keep us in your light that the darkness of evil
    may not engulf us so that, on our journey through life,
    we may always be children of the light, filled with
    confidence in your love and power.   **Amen**

A Litany of Thanksgiving (*Based on Isa. 63.7*)

Let us recount the Lord's unfailing love:
**He has cared for his people despite our unworthiness
throughout the ages.**
Let us recount the prowess of the Lord:
He is mighty and victorious, the ruler of all.
Let us remember all that God has done for us:
**From the first to the last the Lord has been gracious to his whole
creation.**
Let us recount how great has been his goodness to the house of
Israel:
**He brought them out of slavery, taught them the commandments
for life and gave them the Promised Land.**
Let us remember what he has done in his tenderness:
**Like a loving parent God has comforted and cared for us in our
pain and suffering.**
Let us retell his many acts of faithful love:
**He created the world and all that is in it.
He sent his Son to save us from evil and death.
He poured out his Holy Spirit, our advocate and guide.
He is present with us still and knows us by name.**

Let us remember with thanksgiving how great is our God:
   **Glory to the Father, and to the Son
   and to the Holy Spirit;
   as it was in the beginning, is now
   and shall be for ever.   Amen**

Offering Prayer

Jesus Christ, you gave everything for us,
dying that we might live.
We offer these our gifts, and with them ourselves,
so that through us and the work of this church
others may share in your risen life.   **Amen**

Dismissal

The light is among you still.
Go in the light of Christ,
   to serve him with your lives
   and to glorify his name.   **Amen**

Sunday before Easter
Lent 6   Palm Sunday

Presentation

*Palm can have three meanings – obviously, today, the palm trees of
Jerusalem, but also the palm of our hand, and, in some parts of the
country, the 'new-life' shown by buds on the trees. All three can be
woven into a presentation which includes the making of crosses. A
cross made up of cut-out hands, with each person's name written on
them, could be a focus for prayer.*

Call to Worship   *Either Hebrews 10.19–25 Or:*

Like the crowd who shouted 'Hosanna',
   we offer our praise.
Like the crowd who waved their palm branches,
   we offer our worship.
Like Jesus, who rode on a donkey,
   we come humbly into the house of God.

Prayer of Confession

Young hands, old hands, fervent hands and hesitant hands,
   all held aloft their palm branches and 'Hosanna' rang out.
Lord, forgive us when we raise our hands, not in praise but in
   despair.
May we know your hands upholding us today.

Strong hands, weak hands, loyal hands and betraying hands,
   all accepted the broken bread from the Master's hand.
Lord, forgive us when we take but do not give.
May we see your hands reaching out to us in acceptance.

Foreign hands, familiar hands, working hands and sad hands,
   all shared in crucifying the son of God.
Lord, forgive us when we have a hand in things that are evil.
May we know your hands outstretched in love.   **Amen**

Prayer for Holy Week

*Seated, quietly sing verse 1 of
'Were you there when they crucified my Lord?'*

Lord God, we know that the joy and celebration
of Palm Sunday were soon overshadowed by the sad events of the
following week.
Help us to remember:
- Maundy Thursday, when, after supper, Jesus prayed in
  the garden and was arrested.   *Silence*
- The anguish of the trial and the terrible feeling when
  the people shouted 'Crucify!'   *Silence*
- The road to Calvary, those who helped Jesus, and the
  soldiers who, only doing their duty, crucified him.   *Silence*

Sing verse 2
Help us to remember:
- those who hung on either side of Jesus.   *Silence*
- those who carefully took Jesus' body down and laid it
  in the tomb.   *Silence*

Sing verse 3
Lord God, as we go through this Holy Week and remember all
that happened to your Son, may his selfless, obedient example
inspire us to offer our lives for you, so that we may share in the
joy of his resurrection.   **Amen**

Prayer of selfless obedience

God called to Abraham,
   'Take your son, offer him as a sacrifice'.
Your commands are often so demanding
that they challenge our faith and trust.
You send us where we would not choose to go.
You ask us to do things which are contrary to our wishes.
You set us tasks which seem as hard as climbing mountains.
Yet, in the self-giving of Jesus,
you made a sacrifice for us.
May we always be willing to give ourselves for you.   **Amen**

Blessing

Blessed is the one who goes in the name of the Lord.
Blessed is the one who is consecrated by the Lord.
Blessed is the one who proclaims the Lord's glory.
Blessed be you who are marked with the sign of the cross.

Easter Day

Presentation

*To many people, and especially children, Easter means 'eggs'. Take
this image of new life and explore its significance throughout the
service. A bare cross with multi-coloured fabrics arranged fan-like
behind it illustrates the glory of empty cross and resurrection.
The Isaiah passage is long for all-age worship, so use selected verses.
The epistle could introduce Holy Communion. The John passage
could be re-enacted using several voices or read in sections at
different points in the service.*

Call to Worship

L: The Lord is risen!   R: **He is risen indeed!**

L: Lift up your heads you gates: R: **Let the king of glory enter**.
L: The Lord is our strength: R: **and has become our salvation**.
L: Christ is our Passover Lamb: R: **who died and rose for us**.
L: The Lord is risen!   R: **He is risen indeed!**
L: He is the Resurrection: R: **He is the Life**.
L: He is the first and the last: R: **He is the living one**.
L: The Lord is risen!   R: **He is risen indeed!**

If used last week, sing verse 4 of 'Were you there . . .?'

Prayer of Adoration

Living God,
    we worship you today with joy in our hearts,
    for when the powers of evil had done their
    worst you raised your Son to life again,
    giving hope to the world.
Alleluia! **Alleluia!**
Lord Jesus Christ,
    we rejoice that you were raised to life and
    that you are alive for evermore. You greeted
    your friends in the garden and on the beach,
    and now you stand among us in your risen power.
Alleluia! **Alleluia!**

Holy Spirit,
  you are always giving new life to the people of
  God. Shape us in the image of Christ, fill us
  with his love, strengthen us by your presence.
Alleluia! **Alleluia!**   **Amen**

Prayer of Intercession   *Based on a Namibian child's prayer*

Gentle Jesus, be with us today.
  We ask that you will give us everything we need.
Gentle Jesus, be with all those in hospital.
  We ask that you will give them strength.
Gentle Jesus, be with all parents and families.
  We ask that you will help them in their relationships.
Gentle Jesus, be with those who are sad.
  We ask that you will let them know you care.
Gentle Jesus, be with those who feel alone or unwanted.
  We ask that you will let them know you are near.
Gentle Jesus, be with us as we talk with you in our prayers, and
for evermore.   **Amen**

Final Prayer

Lord Jesus, you are the conqueror of death. You came alive from
the tomb to be our Saviour. Peter and John discovered an empty
grave. You spoke to Mary by name and she recognized you by
your voice. Then you appeared to all your disciples. Be with us in
all our darkness and insecurity. Help us to understand the
message of the empty tomb. Speak to us so that we, like Mary,
may recognize your voice. Convince us that you are alive, so that
we too may proclaim that we have 'seen the Lord'.

Dismissal

May the Father raise you to new life,
may the Son go with you throughout your pilgrimage,
and may the Holy Spirit fill you as holy disciples.
Go and announce that 'the Lord is risen!'.   **Amen**

1st Sunday after Easter

Presentation

Faith in a saving God is the central theme of all three readings for today – faith in a God who saves his people from their enemies, and faith in a God who saves us through Christ. The risen Christ appeared to his followers in a locked room. Faith focusses on the spiritual reality of his presence. To the display started before Easter, a key to a locked door could be added, reminding us that the risen Christ is not bound by earthly limitations.

Call to Worship   (*I Peter 1.8*)

Although we have not seen him, yet we love him;
  and trusting in him, we are filled with joy too great
  for words.
Praise to God, the Father of our risen Lord Jesus Christ.

Prayer of Adoration

Praise to our God
– who calls us into life and light,
– who calls us out of nothingness and night.
Alleluia! **Praise to our God. Alleluia!**

Praise to our God
– who formed the earth out of darkness and waste,
– who breathed humanity into man and woman.
Alleluia! **Praise to our God. Alleluia!**

Praise to our God
– who rescued his people from the degradation of slavery,
– who gave them freedom and a life of their own.
Alleluia! **Praise to our God. Alleluia!**

Praise to our God
– who remained faithful to his faithless children,
– who gave his prophets the message of justice and love.
Alleluia! **Praise to our God. Alleluia!**

Praise to our God
- who sent his Son to those living in the darkness of
  sin,
- who sent his Son to suffer for our mistakes.

Alleluia! **Praise to our God. Alleluia!**

Praise to our God
- who raised our glorious Lord Jesus from the dead,
- who has given us a living hope that nothing can
  destroy.

Alleluia! **Praise to our God. Alleluia!   Amen**

Meditation

Lord, I locked the door of my life and mind,
 for I was afraid of what knowing you might mean.
I was afraid that knowing you
 would challenge all my ideas and priorities,
 turn my comfortable life upside down.
I locked the door of my life and mind
 but still you entered
 and shone with the light of truth.

Lord, I locked the door of my life and heart,
 for I was afraid of what loving you might mean.
I was afraid that loving you
 would mean opening myself up to others,
 would mean suffering and pain.
I locked the door of my life and heart,
 but still you entered
 and filled me with the joy of love.

Lord, I locked the door of my life and soul
 for I was afraid of what trusting you might mean.
I was afraid that trusting you
 would mean stepping out into the unknown,
 would mean losing myself in you.
I locked the door of my life and soul,
 but still you entered
 and said 'Peace be with you.'

2nd Sunday after Easter

Presentation

The three readings speak of a new start together – a new start for God's people, a new start for the fisher-disciples, a new start for Christians as they enter into a transformed relationship with God. Jesus shared breakfast with his disciples – on the Easter display place a breakfast, or just a packet of cornflakes – another new start! This will be the last week of the display.

Opening Sentence (*I Peter 1.21*)

Through Christ we have come to trust in God
  who raised him from the dead and gave him glory,
  and so our faith and hope are fixed on God.

Prayer of Confession and Renewal

When we grow tired of trying to do what is right, Lord:
Help us to make a fresh start.

When a friendship or relationship is broken, Lord:
Help us to make a fresh start.

When we have stopped telling others of your love, Lord:
Help us to make a fresh start.

When we have lost our sense of self-respect, Lord:
Help us to make a fresh start.

When our faith in you grows weak, Lord:
Help us to make a fresh start.

Unchanging God, your love for us is new each day.
Every day you call us to turn to you, that you may renew our lives. We confess that our loving grows tired, our faith static, our hope stale. Forgive us and transform us,
for the sake of your Son, Jesus Christ, who died and rose again that all might be made new.   **Amen**

Prayers of Intercession

Lord, we pray for the humble,
for all who feel powerless, oppressed,
and of little account in the world, for . . .
Lord, we pray that, in the power of your Spirit,
we may bring good news to the humble and poor.

Lord, we pray for the broken-hearted,
for those whose lives have been shattered,
whose hopes dashed yet again, for . . .
Lord, we pray that, in the power of your Spirit,
we may be a strong support to the broken-hearted.

Lord, we pray for the captive,
for those in prison, those confined to home or bed,
for . . .
and those imprisoned by their own fears and weaknesses.
Lord, we pray that, in the power of your Spirit,
we may proclaim the true liberty of the children of God.

Lord, we pray for those who mourn,
for all who feel the loss of what they have loved;
a person, a way of life, a physical ability, for . . .
Lord, we pray that, in the power of your Spirit,
we may be of comfort to all who mourn.

In the name of Jesus, the Christ, the Anointed One, who came to
bring the good news of salvation to all the earth. **Amen**

Dismissal and Blessing

God the Creator has made you,
God the Son has saved you,
God the Holy Spirit has made you holy.
Go out into the world, renewed and refreshed,
to serve the God of love in obedience and trust.
May the blessing of God, Father, Son and Spirit,
go with you.

3rd Sunday after Easter

Presentation

*The three readings reflect on the relationship between God and his
people and on our proper response to God as being one of love – with
the love of a bride for her husband, with a love that involves service
and suffering, with a love that is anything but lukewarm. Discuss with
the congregation ways in which we show our love for God, and turn
their suggestions into a prayer of dedication.*

Call to Worship

In love, let us worship and adore our God.
In love, let us listen to his word for us.
In love, let us offer our lives to him.
We love, because he first loved us.

Prayer

Love spoke,
  and creation came into being.
Love spoke,
  and everything came from nothing.
Love speaks, saying, 'Love me,
  and you will know
  the love at the heart of the universe.'
L: God of love: R: **We adore you**.

Love spoke
  in parables and words of hope and healing.
Love spoke forgiveness
  to those who were condemned and despised.
Love speaks, saying, 'Love me,
  and you will know
  the saving love that is real life.'
L: God of love: R: **We adore you**.

Love spoke
  in fiery words that all could understand.
Love spoke good news
  to the lost and loveless.

Love speaks, saying, 'Love me,
   and you will know
   that I live within your heart.'
L: God of love: R: **We adore you**.

Father, Son and Holy Spirit,
   we love and adore you. **Amen**

Prayers of Intercession

Let us pray for a world hungry for justice and
freedom from warfare, oppression and want. We pray for . . .
L: Lord, we love you: R: **Help us to feed your sheep**.

Let us pray for a society hungry for a sense of community, where
many feel worthless and uncared for, and respect for others is in
short supply. We pray for . . .
L: Lord, we love you: R: **Help us to feed your sheep**.

Let us pray for a church hungry for a vision for the future, where
too often commitment is lukewarm and a sense of direction
missing. We pray for . . .
L: Lord, we love you: R: **Help us to feed your sheep**.

Let us pray for one another. We each have a particular hunger in
our lives. We pray for the lonely, the anxious, the bereaved, and
those sick in body, mind or spirit.
We pray for . . .
L: Lord, we love you: R: **Help us to feed your sheep**.
In the name of Christ, the Good Shepherd. **Amen**

Dismissal

Go out in love, warmed by God,
To warm the lives of those you meet.
Go out with the fiery blessing of the Lord.

4th Sunday after Easter

Presentation

A saving relationship with God comes not from an unthinking observance of religious rules and practices, but from hearts and lives turned towards him. Such holiness can come as a reproach or threat to others, and arouse antagonism and hatred.

Tell the story of a modern martyr like Martin Luther King or Oscar Romero showing how their convictions, rooted in their relationship with God, involved them in confrontation.

Call to Worship   (*Ezek. 36.23,26,28*)

'I am the Lord,' says the Lord God.
'I shall give you a new heart
   and put a new spirit within you.'
'You will be my people and I shall be your God.'

Prayer of Confession

Lord our God, we turn to you,
   seeking forgiveness for the many times
   when the fruit of your spirit has been lacking
   from our lives.

We have not shown love to others but been more concerned
   with our own wants and comfort.
L: Lord, give us a new heart: R: **Put a new spirit within us**.

We have lost all sense of joy and peace and become
   submerged in anxiety and fear.
L: Lord, give us a new heart: R: **Put a new spirit within us**.

We have not been patient or kind but found it difficult
   to cope with the failings of others.
L: Lord, give us a new heart: R: **Put a new spirit within us**.

We have despaired of being good and have disloyally
   compromised with the values of the world.
L: Lord, give us a new heart: R: **Put a new spirit within us**.

We have lacked gentleness and self-control,
   putting our own feelings before those of others.
L: Lord, give us a new heart: R: **Put a new spirit within us**.

Loving God, we do not have the power to transform ourselves.
But through your crucified and risen Son, you have offered us
forgiveness and a new life. Lord, fill us with your Spirit, that we
may truly become your people.
   We ask this through Christ's name.   **Amen**

Meditation

Lord, why do we hate goodness so much?

Why does the thought of goodness attract us,
   but its reality make us withdraw
   into our invulnerable shells.

We see a good deed done
   and immediately start to question the motives of the doer.

We hear a woman speak out on behalf of goodness
   and her demands strike fear into our heart.
   We long for her to be silenced.

We do not learn, Lord,
   for this is what the world did to you:
   questioned your motives, hated your words,
   tried to destroy goodness by killing you.

Lord, you broke out of the tomb.
Break into our shells and free us.
Open us up to your goodness.

Dismissal   (*Gal. 5.25*)

The Spirit is the source of your life.
Let the Spirit also direct its course.

5th Sunday after Easter

Presentation

The readings this week continue to look at the nature of our relationship with God and through them we trace the development of that relationship – from the mediation of Moses and the revealing work of Jesus to Paul's triumphant assertion that 'nothing can separate us from the love of God'. To illustrate an aspect of mediation, have a piece of 'gobbledegook', legal or insurance company jargon, read out, followed by a translation into plain English. Ask the congregation how they would explain words like 'salvation', 'repentance', 'holiness' etc. to someone outside the church tradition.

Opening Sentence *(Rom. 8.32)*

If God is on our side, who is against us?
He did not spare his own Son, but gave him up for us all;
how can he fail to lavish every other gift upon us?

Prayer of Adoration and Thanksgiving

Lord God Almighty,
   King of the Universe,
   Author of creation,
   who dwell in the searing light of glory,
   who make your home in the darkness of mystery,
   who is holiness and majesty and power,
   we worship you.

We worship you with reverence
   and we worship you with thankfulness
   that you have come to your people
   and made yourself known to us.

We thank you that you have spoken to us
   through Moses and the prophets,
   revealing yourself as a faithful,
   just and righteous God.

We thank you that your Word came to us,
   as Jesus Christ, your only Son,
   revealing yourself as a forgiving,
   loving and gracious God.

We thank you that you still speak to us
   through the Bible, through the prayers and words of
   others, through the wonders of your creation,
   assuring us of your strength, beauty and love.

Lord God Almighty,
   King of the Universe,
   author of creation,
   you have given yourself to us
   and promised us that nothing can take us away from you.

God of love,
   we worship you.   **Amen**

Prayer of Dedication

Loving God, you have given yourself to us;
now we offer ourselves to you.

Yes, Lord, we accept your offer of love and forgiveness.
Yes, Lord, we will follow you.
Yes, Lord, we will give to you all that we have and are.

We long for others to know you, God,
   to share our joy and peace and hope,
   to find the path to eternal life.

Take us, God, and use us,
   fill us with your Spirit
   that we may be
   messengers of your good news for all,
   guides on the pilgrim way of life.
In the name of Jesus Christ, your Word for us.   **Amen**

Dismissal

Go out with confidence and joy,
   for Christ has conquered the world.

6th Sunday after Easter

Sunday after Ascension Day

Presentation

The earthly Christ is affirmed as being of God, and must take his rightful place with God in order for the Holy Spirit to enter into the lives of his followers.

The Ascension asserts that Christ is the Son of God and that, in the divine plan, loss is turned into gain.

Ask the congregation to suggest different titles for Christ, and turn this into a meditative prayer of adoration, with silence interspersed with the words:

'Jesus, (*title*), you are worthy of all praise'.

The II Kings reading could be enacted in mime or dance.

Call to Worship   (*Rev. 5.13b*)

'Praise and honour, glory and might,
to him who sits on the throne and to the Lamb forever.'

Prayer of Thanksgiving

Let us offer our thanks to God, the creator,
    for the world in which we live,
    for its beauty, its balance and its bounty,
    and for making men and women,
    that we may seek and know and love him.
L: For the gift of life: R: **Thanks be to God**.

Let us offer our thanks to God, the gracious one,
    for the gift of the Son, Jesus Christ,
    who emptied himself of all but love,
    to bring the good news of forgiveness to the world
    and who reigns again with God in glory.
L: For the gift of Christ: R: **Thanks be to God**.

Let us offer our thanks to God, the life-giver,
    for the gift of the Holy Spirit,
    who sweeps into the lives of Christ's followers,
    filling them with love, peace and joy,
    giving them courage and comfort and guidance.
L: For the gift of the Holy Spirit: R: **Thanks be to God.**   **Amen**

Offering Prayer

Father God, who sent your Son into the world
and received him again to your throne in heaven,
we thank you for all that you have given to us
and offer these gifts of money as tokens cf ourselves.
Accept them and us in the service of your kingdom.   **Amen**

Prayers of Intercession

Tell the congregation to expect periods of silence

God of wisdom,
we pray for those leaders of the nations who have lost
sight of the vision of a just and peaceful world.
Silence
Lord, send your Spirit to open their eyes
to a vision of the kingdom of love.

God of wholeness, we pray for a church struggling to offer
a glimpse of Christ in a changing and materialistic world.
Silence
Lord, send your Spirit to enrich our faith
and empower our words and actions.

God of love, we pray for all who feel that they have lost
sight of Christ, through sorrow, sickness, anxiety or
doubt.
Silence
Lord, send your Spirit to breathe new life
into those who despair and comfort them
with the knowledge of your presence.
In the name of our risen and ascended Saviour,
Jesus Christ.   **Amen**

Dismissal

Go, live and love in the power of the Spirit,
for the ascended Christ is with you until the end of time.

Pentecost

Presentation

*God brings to life what, to human eyes, seems totally dead. The Holy
Spirit comes like a breath of fresh air to cleanse, heal and renew, to
bring new life. The Holy Spirit came 'as the wind'. We can hear and
feel the wind and notice its effect but we cannot see it. Ask people to
blow on to their hands or use a fan to blow some paper or cloth, as
you speak about the Holy Spirit. Blow up some balloons to show
wind at work. The church could be bedecked in red and white, the
colours of Pentecost.*

Call to Worship   *(John 3.8)*

'The wind blows where it will; you hear the sound of it, but you
do not know where it comes from or where it is going. So it is
with the Holy Spirit.'
May the Spirit of God, powerful as a desert wind, refreshing as a
summer breeze, inspire our worship today.

Prayer of Praise and Thanksgiving

L: Lord, your Spirit is with us, breathing new life into
   our hearts and minds, and for that we praise you:
R: **We praise you and thank you, Lord**.
L: Lord, your Spirit is with us, showing us the way to
   live, and for that we praise you:
R: **We praise you and thank you, Lord**.
L: Lord, your Spirit is with us, giving us the love,
   courage and power to be your witnesses, and for that
   we praise you:
R: **We praise you and thank you, Lord**.
L: Lord, your Spirit is with us, helping us in our
   struggles and strengthening us to face the day,
   and for that we praise you:
R: **We praise you and thank you, Lord**.
O Holy Spirit, forgive us when we lose confidence in you and
think you have gone away and left us. Help us never to forget
that you live in us and work through us, as you bring life to the
world.   **Amen**

Prayer of Commitment

O Holy Spirit of God, help us not to be confined by these
buildings, but lead us out into the world.
We commit ourselves, in the power of the Holy Spirit, to share
your love with our neighbours and friends.
We commit ourselves to respond, in word and action, to all in
need, and especially to the hungry, the homeless, and the
friendless. We go in the name of Jesus Christ.   **Amen**

Prayer of Intercession

Let us pray for the work of the Holy Spirit in the world;
– where there is war and bloodshed;   *Silence*
– where there is famine and hunger;   *Silence*
– where people cannot speak freely and worship openly;   *Silence*
– where violence dominates communities and people live
   in fear for their lives;   *Silence*
O Holy Spirit, bring to these places of suffering renewed hope
and a vision of peace and justice for all.

Let us pray for the work of the Holy Spirit in the church:
– where there seems to be no future or sign of renewal;   *Silence*
– where worship is dull and lacking in inspiration;   *Silence*
– where fellowship is weak and there is little warmth
   among the people;   *Silence*
– where strangers are not made to feel at home;   *Silence*
O Holy Spirit, bring to these places a renewed sense of purpose
and the vision of a church in which God is active, and a church at
work in the lives of all people.

O Holy Spirit, you breathe life into dry bones;
   you reveal the truth about God;
   you bring the deepest peace and most perfect love.
May today be a Pentecost for us,
   set our hearts and minds, bodies and souls ablaze with
   the inspiration of the Holy Spirit so that the prayers we
   bring may not be empty words but fire us to action.   **Amen**

1st Sunday after Pentecost
Trinity Sunday

Isa. 40.12–17
I Tim. 6.11–16
John 14.8–17

Presentation

The God who seems a long way away and to whom the nations mean nothing (Isaiah in REB) is the same God who can be seen and known in Jesus (John). He is the God who is revealed through the Holy Spirit in the Christian and who helps life's race to be run and won (I Timothy). Ask the congregation to think of a person with whom they have a close relationship – maybe a friend, parent, grand-parent, partner. Has the relationship always been close or has it grown close over time? How has it grown? Through doing things together? Through a crisis? Through enjoying common interests? Through talking and sharing together? All or some of these? Does our relationship with God grow in a similar or different way? Prepare a focus for worship with items from the world around us which remind us of a growing relationship with God and help us to express it.

Call to Worship

Let us worship God the Father who out of love created us.
    God the Son who out of love saves us.
    God the Holy Spirit who out of love lives in us.

Prayer of Adoration

God – Father, Mother, Parent, Friend – you can seem a long way away from us, lost in the vastness of your creation, outside of time, above space, beyond our understanding. Yet out of love for us you sent Jesus into our time and space to be one of us, to share our humanity, with its joy and pain, happiness and suffering, togetherness and loneliness. And, through the Holy Spirit, you are always with us, as Jesus promised, helping us to love you and to follow you all the days of our life.
L: We praise you, O God: R: **We adore and worship you**.
We thank you for the many ways in which we can see you
– in the beauty and wonder of your creation,
– in the love of parents and friends, brothers and sisters,
– in music, art and literature,
– and in your many gifts, given day by day.
L: We praise you, O God: R: **We adore and worship you.**   **Amen**

Prayer of Confession

Confession is not just about saying sorry and asking for forgiveness but about making a new start and going in a different direction. This is reflected in these prayers.

Lord our God, Father, creator of all things beautiful:
forgive us for the way we treat your world.
For failing to keep it clean, for polluting its rivers and streams,
for leaving litter when we should take it home, please forgive us
and help us to mend our ways.
L: We are sorry we have let you down:
R: **Help us to start again**.

Lord our God, Father of Jesus our Saviour: forgive us for failing
to love our neighbours and friends with the love Jesus showed us,
for not welcoming strangers from other cultures, races and
communities, for closing our eyes to the needs of others and for
putting ourselves first.
L: We are sorry we have let you down:
R: **Help us to start again**.

Lord our God, sender of the Holy Spirit to guide and lead us into
all truth: forgive us for abusing many of the gifts she brings, for
not cherishing the hallmarks of the Spirit – love, joy and peace –
and for not letting them speak through our lives. Forgive us for
spreading gossip, bringing division, telling lies.
L: We are sorry we have let you down:
R: **Help us to start again**.

Lord, you forgive us as we forgive others.
Help us not to hold grudges against other people,
but to be gracious to those who have harmed us
and loving to those who would hate us.
Help us never to be embittered but always to strive for the best
and to see the best in others.
We can only do these things with your help.
May the Holy Spirit fill our lives with the love of Jesus.   **Amen**

2nd Sunday after Pentecost

Presentation

Read John in three 'parts'; narrator, Nicodemus and Jesus, the narrator standing away from the other two.

Paragraphs in the prayer of thanksgiving and intercession can be read by different people.

Call to Worship

God calls us together to worship.
> Let us bring all that we have and all that we are.
> Let us be renewed by the Spirit.
> Let us worship the Lord our God.

Prayer of Thanksgiving and Intercession

We praise you, O God, and give you thanks for all those who proclaim the good news of Jesus Christ – that your love is for all people.
We thank you for all who express your word in daily life:
> in their homes and where they spend their leisure;
> in their service to the community and where they work;
> in factory, office, shop, school or hospital.
We thank you for ministers and for all who hear and obey
> your call to be *local preachers* and leaders of worship.
And we pray for this congregation
> that, in worship, we may share our gifts of making
> music, singing, acting, dancing, reading and praying;
and that, in witness, we may support each other,
> welcoming the stranger and encouraging all who are
> anxious, distressed or bereaved.

It is daunting, Lord, to be called to carry the good news into the whole world. May the promise of Jesus reassure us and his presence give us strength. May our words and actions proclaim your truth and express your love wherever there is need.   **Amen**

Meditation and Prayer of Petition

Lord, you say that we have to be born again.
But how is it possible?
Nicodemus asked if he could enter his mother's womb a second
time, but he didn't really expect an answer.
The idea was ridiculous.

You say that we have to be born of the Spirit.
Isn't flesh and blood good enough?
Aren't we fully human when we are born?
You say that it is only when we are born of water and spirit that
we can enter the Kingdom of God.
But we thought that the Kingdom of God was within us!
What did you mean when you spoke to Nicodemus in the middle
of the night?
When something is born, it is new – a baby, a flower, an idea.
We can understand that something, once new, may need to be
renewed. A car may need a new engine, or an arthritic hip a new
plastic joint.
And we know that forgiveness can transform human lives.
Is this what you mean, Lord, by being born again?
That your Spirit can renew our lives, replacing selfishness by self-
giving and turning hatred into love?
Is this what you mean by being born again?
That our lives can be turned upside down
and given a new start and a new meaning?

Lord, take our lives and renew us.
Take our worship and make it vital.
Take our service and bring it alive with your love.
Blow Spirit, like the wind, and make all things new.   **Amen**

Dismissal

Go, and live a new life, filled with God's Spirit.
Go, and serve the Lord, in the power of his love.
Go, and serve others, in Jesus' name.   **Amen**

3rd Sunday after Pentecost

Presentation

*Two themes from the readings are 'faithfulness' and 'being a witness
to the truth about God'. Jesus bore witness to God's truth. Christians
are called to lead faithful lives and, in doing so, are themselves
witnesses to God's truth.*

*Using a flip chart or board, ask the congregation to share ideas of
what 'faithfulness' and 'witness' mean. Have symbols (eg. wedding
ring) to represent these ideas. Interview someone about being a
witness to something they saw, or ask them to tell part of their
Christian story or to say how another's witness influenced their lives.*

Call to Worship

L: This is the day which the Lord has made:
R: **Let us rejoice and be glad in it**.
L: This is the day to celebrate God's love:
R: **Let us give thanks and praise**.
L: This is the day to sing and speak God's truth:
R: **Let us worship the Lord our God with body, mind
and spirit**.

Prayer of Praise and Thanksgiving

We praise you, Lord, for those who have been your faithful
witnesses down the ages, for saints and martyrs, for preachers
and prophets, for unsung Christians of every age.

We thank you for the example they give to us, for their
faithfulness and endurance, for their love of Christ and their
commitment to people in need.

We praise you for people of every race, culture and language,
united with us in Christ despite their different practice and
tradition.

We thank you that you call women and men to serve you
faithfully and to witness to the truth of God found in Jesus
Christ.

We praise you that, as we follow in the great procession of
witnesses who have gone before us and as we prepare the way for
those who will come after, you help us to keep the faith. Help us,
remembering all that Christ has made possible, to rely on his
grace and strength as we witness to our own generation.   **Amen**

Prayer of Confession

Lord Jesus Christ, who took the road to Jerusalem
knowing that it was the way to the cross,
forgive us for wanting to take the easy road.
We have been selfish and thoughtless, and our words have been
hasty and our actions insensitive;
we have kept our faith to ourselves, and our discipleship has cost
us little.
Forgive us that, in all these ways, we have caused you pain and
failed our neighbours.
And give us the courage to take up our cross and follow you.
L: Lord, in your mercy: R: **Hear our prayer**.

We have been faithless, but Jesus, who was faithful to the end,
speaks to us of God's mercy and love and offers us forgiveness.
Hear his words to those who repent and put their trust in him:
'Your sins are forgiven'.   **Amen**

Before the Prayers of Intercession

L: Give us a vision, Lord: R: **A vision of peace in our time**.
L: Help us to see, Lord: R: **To see a world in need**.
L: Give us a picture, Lord: R: **Of what we can do to bring love,
                                 joy and peace**.
L: Give us a vision, Lord: R: **As we offer our prayers of
                                 intercession**.

Dismissal

Go into the world, knowing that Christ goes with you,
and share with others the light of his truth,
whose faithfulness endures for ever.   **Amen**

4th Sunday after Pentecost

Micah 4.1–7
Heb. 12.18–29
John 4.5–26

Presentation

There is a common theme of worshipping God in spirit and in truth.
John offers insights into the breaking down of the barriers between
people of different races and faiths. This text could be dramatized or
read by three voices. A bowl or pitcher of water would add visual
impact. Ask the congregation to share how water brings life and
refreshment. God, through Jesus, gives the water of life.

Call of Worship

We come to worship in the Lord's house.
Let us lift up our hearts and voices in praise.
Let us worship in spirit and in truth.
Let us give God all honour and glory.

Prayer of Confession

Water: crystal clear, shining bright, bringing refreshment
    to parched travellers, new life to barren land.
Yet water: so often polluted and destroyed by our
    unthinking and uncaring ways, so often used as a
    dumping ground for our waste.
Water: gushing torrents, idling rivers, thundering water-
    falls, sparkling in the sunlight, bringing coolness to
    tired feet, delight to young children as they splash
    and play.
Yet water: a source of power capable of great destruction
    as well as being an oasis in the desert;
    a gift to be gathered and used, not wasted and abused.
Water: the essence of life in every drop, by which we are
    baptized and brought into God's family, through which
    we are cleansed and healed.

Forgive us, Lord, for forgetting that this is your gift,
    created at the beginning of time.
Forgive us for polluting the rivers and seas,
    for making a mockery of your generosity.

Forgive us for turning rivers red with the blood of the
    victims of war and hatred.
Forgive us for failing to drink refreshing,
    life-giving water, the channel of your grace.
Forgive us for taking for granted this precious gift.
May your living water give us the power to follow your way all
the days of our life.   **Amen**

Prayers of Intercession

I ask your prayers for people and places:
- where there is war, fighting and bloodshed;
- where life has been uprooted and devastated;
- where death is common-place and the burial of sons and
  daughters, mothers and fathers, friends and relatives
  a daily occurrence.

The congregation is invited to name such places
L: Lord, in your mercy: R: **Hear our prayer**.

I ask your prayers
- for those who work for peace and justice;
- for individuals and organizations who give time
  and energy in the search for lasting peace;
- who put their own lives at risk for the sake of others.

The congregation is invited to name such people
L: Lord, in your mercy: R: **Hear our prayer**.

I ask your prayers
- for those who seek to break down the barriers between
  peoples of different races and faiths;
- for those who seek to build up trust,
  understanding and mutual respect.

The congregation is invited to name such people
L: Lord, in your mercy: R: **Hear our prayer**.

Lord God, lover of all, who longs to see the end of war,
bitterness and mistrust, we commit to your care all whom we
have named, all who work for the healing of the nations and for
peace, justice and reconciliation between communities. May they
know your strength and grace that they may do your will.   **Amen**

Jonah (3.6–10), 4.1–11
Eph. 2.11–22
John 4.27–42

5th Sunday after Pentecost

Presentation

Hope is a dominant theme in the readings – for the people of Nineveh (Jonah), the Samaritans (John), and for all humanity (Ephesians). Dramatize the Jonah reading as a conversation between him and God (like the meditation below). Ask the congregation to explore the meaning of the word 'hope'.

What do they see as signs of hope today?

Call to Worship

Members of God's household, welcome!
Let us worship, not as strangers but as friends,
not as foreigners but as fellow-citizens,
with all God's people in union with Christ Jesus.

Reflective Prayer of Intercession and Petition

Gracious God,
  we reflect on the enmity in the world – far away and near to
  home. We think of places where there is bitterness, and people
  who carry burdens of hate. We bring to mind . . .   *Silence*
Then we remember that you are the peace of the world and you
stand at the centre of all human life.

Gracious God,
  we reflect on the hopelessness of many situations, where there
  seems to be no way out of the traps of poverty and hunger. We
  bring to mind . . .   *Silence*
Then we remember that you are the hope of the world and you
stand at the centre of all human life.

Gracious God,
  We reflect on the despair and loneliness in the world, where
  people can see no future because of unemployment, or
  homelessness, or being a refugee, or a breakdown in
  relationships. We bring to mind . . .   *Silence*
Then we remember that you are the joy of the world and you
stand at the centre of all human life.

Jesus Christ, who came to proclaim the good news of the
Kingdom of God, and to create a new humanity, help us to know
and to share your peace, hope and joy.   **Amen**

Meditation   *Preferably two voices*

God, I was angry when I heard the news this morning.

You know what it was about . . . the fighting in . . .
Why don't you do something to stop it?
Bang a few heads together, make people see sense!
Stop the bullets and impose peace!

You know what it was about . . . the drought in . . .
all that suffering and people dying of hunger.
Why don't you send some rain, or start a river, or change the
weather to allow more crops to grow?
Come on God, get your act together! Do something!

You know what it was about . . . spoiling the environment . . .
the oil spilling into the sea, the air pollution from power stations,
the cutting down of more trees, exploitation of the land for quick
gain – no one caring about the future.
Why don't you stop such foolish people? Make them see the
damage they are doing! Force them to change their minds!

God, it makes me so angry! Why don't people care?
I'm just a mere mortal, no one will listen to me,
I can't change anything, but you can.

(And God replied)
Why should you be angry? How do you think I feel when I see
the world being destroyed? The world I created for all people to
enjoy. A world to reflect my glory.
And I created you – not to opt out but to be involved, and to
show my love. Only through love will people change. Only with
my love will they see a better way.
Go on, use your energy to get things changed!
Get stuck in!

6th Sunday after Pentecost

Presentation

We are surrounded by new life, even in the presence of death. The two healings (John and Acts) bear witness to Jesus as the giver of life. New life is not just for individuals but also for nations (Hosea): renewal through forgiveness and wholeness through faith. Invite people to share their experiences of healing (not only from illness) and new life. Ask in advance to give time for preparation.

Prayer of Praise and Thanksgiving

L: For all the beauty of your creation, and for the
newness each season brings.
For signs of new life:

R: **We thank and praise you**.

L: For springtime, with bulbs, buds and blossom bursting out.
For signs of new life:

R: **We thank and praise you**.

L: For summer, sunny days, fresh air and holidays.
For signs of new life:

R: **We thank and praise you**.

L: For autumn, colours of brown and gold, the harvest of
farm, orchard and sea.
For signs of new life:

R: **We thank and praise you**.

L: For winter, rain and frost to renew the soil, snow
making everything white.
For signs of new life:

R: **We thank and praise you**.

L: But most of all, for eternal life in Jesus Christ who helps us to
see the world through God's eyes, and to live in God's way.
For signs of new life:

R: **We thank and praise you.   Amen**

Prayers of Intercession

Let us pray for the healing of the nations –
   places of suffering and despair . . . conflict and
   bitterness . . . countries at war . . .
   We pray for the peacemakers and for those who
   try and show a different way to live.
L: Lord, for those in need of healing:
R: **Bring renewal and hope**.

Let us pray for the healing of the nations –
   places where people of different races and cultures are
   suspicious of each other . . . of industry and commerce where
   conflicting interests threaten everyone's livelihood . . .
   We pray for those who seek to bring tolerance, understanding
   and co-operation.
L: Lord, for those in need of healing:
R: **Bring renewal and hope**.

Let us pray for the healing of individuals –
   people whose bodies and minds have been damaged by
   illness, disease, accident or neglect . . . for those
   addicted to drugs or alcohol . . . for those whose
   feelings of guilt are a heavy burden . . .
   We pray for all who help them, doctors and nurses,
   ministers and pastoral workers, who bring the wholeness
   and joy you wish for us all.
L: Lord, for those in need of healing:
R: **Bring renewal and hope**.

Let us pray for our own healing –
   we bring before you our worries and concerns . . .
   strained relationships . . . divisions between Christians . . .
   uncertain faith . . .
   We pray for your love and support, comfort and hope,
   brought to us through the gospel of Christ.
L: Lord, for those in need of healing:
R: **Bring renewal and hope.   Amen**.

Closing words

Go out into the world knowing that God goes with you.
Go out into the world in the power of God's love.
Go out into the world to share the good news of the new life
offered in Jesus Christ.

7th Sunday after Pentecost

Presentation

*In the New Testament lessons Paul and Jesus are both facing charges
and called to give a witness. To tell the 'whole truth' in a legal context
is never easy, even when one is bearing witness to an everyday event.
Act out a surprise 'incident' and ask people what actually happened –
to be witnesses. Christians are called to bear witness to God's love
and his promise of eternal life, and that is not easy either. We never
lack opportunities, on formal occasions or in informal conversa-
tions. But we may be afraid of missing something out, of failing to tell
the 'whole truth' and letting God down. We must never forget that
God is with us and that we can suddenly find, in moments of trial and
testing, that he is guiding what we say. That is good news indeed!*

Call of Worship

Let us honour the Father
  and glory in the miracle of creation.
Let us honour the Son
  and be filled with the wonder of his love.
Let us honour the Holy Spirit
  and receive the power of God to guide our lives.

Prayer

Who is a God like you? Father of time and space,
holding your children with tender and loving hands,
calling, guiding, challenging them to seek you.
You alone are Lord of all that is.

Who is a God like you? Mother of the universe,
cradling your daughters and sons in the crook of your arm,
loving creation as a hen broods over her chicks.
You alone are Lord of all that is.

Who is a God like you? Sister and brother of humankind,
sharing the common life of the world,
entering its grief and pain, its joy and abundance.
You alone are Lord of all that is.

Who is a God like you? Coming to us in Jesus Christ, the Word
made flesh, testifying to the love you have for us,
giving us life which never ends.
You alone are Lord of all that is.

We praise you, Lord God.
We thank you that you know us,
    accept us and receive us as we are.
We thank you that we can know you,
    know you as Love itself.
There is no God like you.   **Amen**

Prayer of Confession

We confess to you, ever loving God,
that we have hidden our discipleship from others and have failed
to share your love with those in need.
We confess that we have used your gifts selfishly
and have failed to take good care of your creation.

Silence

Forgive us, Lord, and grant us a new start and time to make
amends:
– that we may become true witnesses of your love and
    good stewards of your many gifts;
– that we may stand and be counted as faithful followers
    in the footsteps of Jesus Christ.
To him be praise and glory for evermore.   **Amen**

Closing Words

Tell the world that our God reigns.
Tell the world that our God loves.
Tell the world that our God offers life for evermore.
In the name of the Father, Son and Holy Spirit,
Tell the world that you are one of God's children.

8th Sunday after Pentecost

Presentation

A reference to water occurs in each reading. The stories in the New Testament are under-girded by the comment in Isaiah 43.2a. Use a large caption with the words 'Ships are safe in the harbour, but that is not what ships are for.' Being a Christian involves taking risks, but God promises to remain faithful, and will not let us down, even when the going gets rough.

Prayer of Praise and Thanksgiving

O Lord God, we praise you and thank you for creation,
for the world and all its many peoples.
We praise and thank you that despite its vastness
you know each person, each name and every deepest need.
We praise and thank you that we are precious to you,
that you love us and help us to reflect your glory.
O Lord God, at all times and in all places, we praise you.
We thank you for being with us and for being our life-long
friend.   **Amen**

Meditation *To follow John 6*

Sometimes life seems like being on a ship, tossed this way
and that, at the mercy of mountainous waves,
thinking we are going to be washed overboard,
thinking we cannot cope with what is happening to us.
Then we remember the disciples in their boat.
You came to them and shared their journey,
and brought them safely back to land.
We remember St Paul, before he was ship-wrecked.
He was able to break bread, give thanks to you,
and take courage for what lay ahead.
Give us, Lord, that same courage, knowing that you come to
meet us and to share our journey, knowing that you will not let
the waters overwhelm us or the seas flood our lives so that we
drown.

Help us, Lord,
    to know your peace even in the roughest weather,
    to know your joy even in the darkest hour,
    to know your love, now and when we need it most,
    and to take courage when we break bread together.

Prayers of Intercession

Let us pray for the suffering peoples of the world:
 – for nations who have been dispossessed of their lands
   and have nowhere to call their own;
 – for refugees, driven out of their homes through war,
   famine or disease;
 – for the homeless with no roof for shelter
   or no proper bed in which to sleep;
   and for all who seek to put right that which is wrong.
L: Lord, in all places: R: **May your Kingdom come**.

 – for people unjustly imprisoned because of political
   or religious beliefs;
 – for minorities persecuted because they are seen
   as a threat to the state;
 – for people singled out because of the colour of their
   skin, victims of racial violence and harrassment;
   and for all who seek to put right that which is wrong.
L: Lord, in all places: R: **May your Kingdom come**.

 – for those who feel that they have lost their dignity and
   respect through being unemployed;
 – for those caught in the trap of poverty who struggle
   to make ends meet;
 – for people who are lonely and neglected, and for whom
   no one seems to care;
   and for all who seek to put right that which is wrong.
L: Lord, in all places: R: **May your Kingdom come**.

Lord, you know by name all those who suffer through injustice,
oppression, ill-treatment or neglect. Help us to play our part in
the struggle for justice and to care for all who suffer. May we be
identified with your Kingdom and with Christ, who died for all
people. In his name we pray. **Amen**

9th Sunday after Pentecost

Presentation

Warning! Danger! Don't put stumbling blocks in the way of fellow Christians, don't pass judgments on others. Act out of conviction, go for the eternal food, go for peace, build up the common life. These lessons offer vigorous guidance, in these terms, to Christians facing a range of difficult situations. Build a wall of cardboard boxes, with congregational help (Rom. 14.13), and write on them what prevents Christians being united, or what puts people off the church. Also, prepare a focus for worship with items which represent the peace of 'common life' (Rom. 14.19).

Call to Worship

L: Let us worship God:
R: **And give him the glory**.
L: Let us praise the Lord our maker:
R: **With body, mind and spirit**.
L: Let us give him thanks:
R: **And acknowledge him to be our Lord**.

Prayer of Confession   *Shared by two voices*

You tell us to live together in unity and in peace,
    forgive us for causing disharmony and enmity.
You tell us not to pass judgment on one another,
    forgive us for being so critical and feeling superior
    to others.
You tell us to be guided by love in all we do and say,
    forgive us for our harsh tongues and hasty actions.
You tell us to put the interest of others before our own,
    forgive us for being selfish and self-centred.
Silence
Lord God, hear our prayer.
As we confess our sin, let us receive your forgiveness.
It is your desire that we live together in unity and in love. Help us through the power of your Spirit to follow in your way, to know your truth and to share in your life.
Through Jesus Christ our Lord.   **Amen**

Prayers of Intercession

Ideas could be shared before or during the prayer

The Kingdom of God is justice, peace and joy.
Let us pray for those who suffer through injustice;
Invite the congregation to name such people   Silence
Let your Kingdom come.
L: Let justice be established on earth: R: **And let it begin with us.**

The Kingdom of God is justice, peace and joy.
Let us pray for those who have no peace;
Invite the congregation to name such people   Silence
Let your Kingdom come.
L: Let peace be established on earth: R: **And let it begin with us**.

The Kingdom of God is justice, peace and joy.
Let us pray for those who have no joy;
Invite the congregation to name such people   Silence
Let your Kingdom come.
L: Let joy be established on earth: R: **And let it begin with us**.

Creator God, mother and father of all nations,
Jesus Christ, brother and sister to all humanity,
Holy Spirit, source of love within us and bond of love
between us,
God in three persons, you stand with those whose justice, peace
and joy have been destroyed through oppression, neglect or
abuse of power.
Your Kingdom is founded on what is loving, right and good.
Give to us a renewed vision of a world full of your love and a
commitment to the Kingdom which knows no bounds.   **Amen**

Closing Words

Let love be your guide in all you do and let justice be the
watchword by which you stand. Let peace and joy flow through
your lives as you serve the Lord and build up the common life.
In the name of God.   **Amen**

10th Sunday after Pentecost

Presentation

The theme 'Jesus the Bread of Life' makes this an ideal Sunday to celebrate Holy Communion. Alternatively, an Agapē meal can be shared. Other themes, such as the gaining of wisdom and learning, also emerge from the readings. The church can be decorated with symbols of life, including bread, and symbols of learning. It is important to stress that learning is not limited to formal education and can occur in the church and in the local community. Try and persuade individuals to share their experiences of personal growth and discipleship.

Call to Worship

We come to feast on Christ, the Living Bread.
We come to learn the way to follow him.
We come to hear God's word for us today.
Let us worship and adore the one who is Saviour and Lord.

Responsive Prayer of Thanksgiving

L: There is so much to find out in the world, Lord, so much to discover and learn:

R: **Thank you for our enquiring minds and for the gifts and abilities you have given to us**.

L: There is so much to find out in our community, Lord, so much to learn from each other:

R: **Thank you for this congregation, for our local neighbourhood and for the life and experiences we share together**.

L: There is so much to find out from different cultures and faiths, Lord, so much to share in love and respect:

R: **Thank you for the rich mix of people you have placed on this earth and for all they bring to our common life**.

L: There is so much to learn of Jesus, your Son, Lord,
     so much to learn about his way for our life together:
R: **Thank you that in him you have revealed yourself and
     shown us the depth of your love**
All: **In his name we bring our prayers.   Amen**

Prayer of Confession

Jesus Christ, broken bread for the world, you call us to share, in
   your body, the pain and suffering of humankind.
Jesus Christ, living bread for the world, you call us to celebrate,
   in your body, the life of humankind.
Jesus Christ, eternal bread for the world, you call us to share,
   in your body, life for evermore.
Forgive us, Lord, that so often we want the bread for ourselves
and fail to see that it is bread to be shared with all. Jesus Christ,
broken, living, and eternal bread, release us from our selfish
desires and help us to celebrate your life with the whole of
humanity and so join ourselves to you, now and forever.   **Amen**

Antiphonal prayer   *Divide congregation in two*

Leader: Wisdom says, 'Come, eat the food I have prepared
           and taste the wine I have spiced.'
Group 1:   Lord, help us to live with open hearts and minds.
Group 2:   Help us to share our table not only with friends but
           also with strangers.
Group 1:   Help us to share our homes not only with one another
           but also with the homeless.
Group 2:   Help us to share our food not only with those who
           have plenty but also with the hungry.
Group 1:   Help us to share our riches not only with those who
           are already rich but also with the poor.
Group 2:   For this is wisdom.
Group 1:   This is the right way to live.
Group 2:   You, Lord, sent out to the highways and byways for
           people to share in your feast, to eat your food and
           drink your wine.
Group 1:   So, Lord, may we also live in the same way.
Group 2:   Then our lives will be blessed.
Group 1:   Then our hearts will be open.
Group 2:   Then your love will flood in
All: and your name will be praised.   **Amen**

11th Sunday after Pentecost

Presentation

Gideon wanted God to prove his good faith by providing a sign; and Jesus' brothers suggested that he should prove his true identity, to them and to others, by doing 'great things' in Judaea. But Jesus himself, the truly significant 'sign' of God's love, did not come in response to any human requirement, and elements in his ministry, taken into the worship of the church, have become 'symbols', evoking and sustaining faith. It is important, therefore, to illustrate the difference between a 'sign' (e.g. a road sign) and a 'symbol' (e.g. the cross), thus preparing the way for the prayers which follow.

Opening Prayer   *Other suggestions could be shared*

Help us, Lord, to see the signs of your presence in:
– the happy laughter of children at play;
– the joy of people in love;
– the wisdom offered by those of older years;
– the concern of old for young and young for old;
– the sharing of hopes and fears;
– the facing up to illness and distress;
– the fellowship of the Body of Christ, the church;
– the love of God among the people of God;
Lord, through worship, help us to look at life with your eyes and to see the signs of your Kingdom in those we meet.   **Amen**

Prayer of Presence   *Look around the church*

Let us thank God for the symbols in this church.

Bring forward the font or fill it with water
Lord God, we thank you for the water of baptism.
May it always make real to us the new life to which Christ calls us.
We remember with gratitude those who brought us to be baptised, parents, friends, (sponsors,) God-parents, those who have nurtured us in the Christian life, and all who support and encourage us now.
Silence

218

Bring forward bread and wine
Lord God, we thank you for Holy Communion.
May it always make real to us the friendship of Christ.
We remember with gratitude those who have taught us about
Jesus and shown us what life in fellowship with him can be.
Silence

Bring forward a cross
Lord God, we thank you for the cross.
May it always make real to us the self-less obedience of Jesus,
who lived and died for others, and always proclaim to us his risen
power.
We remember with gratitude those who have preached to us the
good news of salvation and shared with us their hope.
Silence

Bring forward a Bible
Lord God, we thank you for the Bible.
May it always draw us into the story of your loving purpose and
make real to us how you revealed yourself in Jesus Christ.
We remember with gratitude those who have made the Bible live
for us and shown us how God speaks through it today.
Silence

Lord God, may we never forget that we, whose lives are enriched
by these tokens of your love, are called to be the Body of Christ.
Help us to be a sign of his presence and a symbol to all that he is
and does, for his name's sake.   **Amen**

Closing Words

When we go out let us look for signs of God's presence:
– in the stranger as well as the friend;
– in the storm as well as the sunshine;
– in the noise as well as the quiet;
Wherever we go, God will be there.

12th Sunday after Pentecost

Presentation

Wisdom, according to the book of Job, is one of the most important gifts. To possess the mind of Christ, to think as he thought, is to possess wisdom. But who has wisdom? Do you have to be born and brought up in the right place? 'Surely the Messiah is not to come from Galilee?' Then Nicodemus is taunted by the Pharisees, 'Are you a Galilean too?' The John passage could be easily and helpfully read in parts.

Call to Worship

We come to worship, people from different places and backgrounds, and each with a different temperament. Yet we are all called to possess the mind of Christ, and be co-workers in God's service. So let us worship the living God with body, mind and spirit.

Prayer of Confession   (*John 7.52*)

'Are you a Galilean too?', they retorted, 'Study the scriptures and you will see that the prophet does not come from Galilee.'

Where are you from? Surely you are not from there!
You speak strangely – can't you speak properly?
We don't say things like that around here.
You don't speak to them, do you? They're not worth it.
No good has ever come from that family!

Lord, forgive us for our prejudices.
Forgive us for not accepting people who are different from us – in race or colour, in language, faith or sexuality.
Forgive us for only being interested in our friends and for wanting a quiet life.
Forgive us, Lord, and help us to face the many forms of prejudice which afflict us. Give us the grace to acknowledge when we are wrong and to change our ways. Give us the mind of Christ, and make us wise enough to live in your way and no other.   **Amen**

Prayer of Petition

Spirit of wisdom,
fill our wills with the will of Christ.
Spirit of truth,
fill our minds with the mind of Christ.
Spirit of faith,
fill our lives with the life of Christ.
Spirit of love,
fill our hearts with the heart of Christ.
Spirit of God,
may the wisdom, truth, faith and love, which come from
Christ, rule our lives this day and always.   **Amen**

Prayers of Intercession   *A framework for prayer*

God of peace,
we pray for those whose lives have been ruined by war
or conflict; especially . . .
L: Help us to play our part in the renewal of peace:
R: **And to serve our neighbours with love and compassion**.

God of creation,
we pray for those whose lives have been ruined by our
exploitation of the environment; especially . . .
L: Help us to play our part in the renewal of creation:
R: **And to serve our neighbours with love and compassion**.

God of hope,
we pray for those whose lives have been ruined through
injustice and discrimination, especially . . .
L: Help us to play our part in the renewal of hope:
R: **And to serve our neighbours with love and compassion**.

Lord, whose will it is that all humanity shall live together in
harmony and love, we pray for your grace to live faithfully in
your kingdom.   **Amen**

13th Sunday after Pentecost

Ex. 34.4–9
Rom. 7.1–6
John 8.3–11

Presentation

God's spirit sets people free to follow the way of Jesus, free from the Law and the condemnation which comes from disobeying the Law. God accepts people with all their imperfections and points them in a new direction.

Acceptance is a key gospel theme and runs through all the readings. Write the Ten Commandments as if on 'tablets of stone'. The Exodus story can be acted out, with someone out of sight speaking God's words.

Call to Worship

This is the House of God, we rejoice in God's presence.
Let us worship our compassionate and faithful Lord.

Prayer of Confession

L: We come to the living God:
R: **With all our faults and failures**.
L: We come to the living God:
R: **To say we are sorry for our sins**.
L: We come to the living God:
R: **Wanting to make a fresh start**.
L: We come to the living God:
R: **Who receives us as we are and tells us to go and sin
   no more**.
L: We come to the living God:
R: **Who helps us live according to the law of Christ,
   the law of love**.
L: Let his grace strengthen and encourage you and be
   assured that your sins are forgiven:
R: **Thanks be to the living God.   Amen**

Prayer of Presence   *(Ex. 34.5)*

'The Lord came down in the cloud, and, as Moses stood there in his presence, he pronounced the name "Lord".'

Gracious Lord,
help us to be as sensitive as Moses to your presence.
He recognized you in the cloud and spoke your name.
May we recognize you wherever you appear to us.

We sense your presence in the sunshine and the rain, in the birds
of the air and the fish of the sea.
You come to us in the flowers and trees, the valleys and
mountain tops.
L: The whole of creation shouts your name:
R: **Blessed be the name of the Lord!**

We sense your presence in the wonders of science and the
discoveries of nature.
You come to us in the vastness of the universe, in the stars and
planets, and in the tiniest grain of sand on the seashore.
L: The whole of creation shouts your name:
R: **Blessed be the name of the Lord!**

We sense your presence in the miracle of a new-born baby.
You come to us in all the precious moments of life, in staying
young and as we grow old, in living and dying, in joy and
sadness.
L: The whole of creation shouts your name:
R: **Blessed be the name of the Lord!**

We sense your presence in the worship.
You come to us in hymns and songs, in readings and preaching,
in prayers and meditations, in bread and wine.
L: The whole of creation shouts your name:
R: **Blessed be the name of the Lord!**

You come to us, Lord, in many guises.
Forgive us when we fail to recognize your presence, in the
suffering face of humanity and in the struggle for life.
You come to us in the poor, the hungry, the homeless and the
prisoner.
Remind us that in serving them we are serving you.
L: The whole of creation shouts your name:
R: **Blessed be the name of the Lord!**   **Amen**

14th Sunday after Pentecost

Presentation

Light is featured in all the readings. Use a candle to symbolize Jesus as the Light of the World. Ask the congregation to think about light; what does it do? It dispels darkness, shows the way. These ideas can be used to examine the themes of travelling and discovery.

Call to Worship   *Based on Eph. 5.19–20*

Let us sing and make music from our hearts to the Lord.
Let us bring to him praise and adoration.
Let us, in the name of our Lord Jesus Christ, give thanks
    every day to God, our creator, sustainer and friend.

Meditation

Sometimes, Lord, I wander around as if I'm in a fog.
I wouldn't be sure which way to go, even if I could see.
It's a bit like being lost in a wilderness.
I've choices to make – about how I'm going to spend the
    rest of my life; what I'm going to do with my time, my
    money, my energy, and the talents of loving and serving.

I'm not always sure about you – do you *really* exist?
And if you do why should that make any difference to me
and the choices I make in life?
All these doubts and questions – are they part of your plan?

'And all the time the Lord went before them;
by day a pillar of cloud to guide them on their journey,
by night a pillar of fire to give them light.'

'Jesus said, "I am the light of the world.
No follower of mine shall walk in darkness." '

Lord, in all my wanderings, be my guide;
    in all my doubts, be my friend;
    in all my questions, be my teacher;
    in all my darkness, be my light.

Prayer of Confession

Forgive us, Lord,
it is so easy to become buried in our own little world.
When we look up and see the pain and suffering of so many, it is
easier not to want to know.
L: Light the darkness, Lord:
R: **Keep our eyes open to the needs of others**.

We see the gaunt faces of the poor, the pot-bellies of the hungry,
the cardboard cities of the homeless, the needle marks of the
addict.
We feel helpless at the sight of such suffering.
Help us not to turn away.
L: Light the darkness, Lord:
R: **Keep our eyes open to the needs of others**.

You made all people in your image.
You tell us to be brothers and sisters to everyone.
You sent your Light that the dark places might be exposed.
Help us not to turn away from the Jesus who lives with those who
suffer in a darkness which seems never ending.
L: Light the darkness, Lord:
R: **Keep our eyes open to the needs of others**.

You challenge us to follow you:
– to go where the light shines in the darkness;
– to give ourselves for the sake of others;
– to live simply and to share what we have.
Help us to make this world your kingdom and by your love,
to bring to an end all fear, misery and suffering.
L: Light the darkness, Lord:
R: **Keep our eyes open to the needs of others**.   **Amen**

Dismissal

Eternal God, behind us, before us, with us,
friend and neighbour, go with us on our journey.   **Amen**

15th Sunday after Pentecost

Presentation

The freedom found in being a child of God is a strong theme in today's readings. Both the gospel and epistle concentrate on individuals being free when they put their trust in God through Jesus Christ. Jeremiah, caught up in the political struggles of his day, believes Israel's liberation from Nebuchadnezzar will come only when the nation keeps God's commandments and ceases to follow false prophets like Hananiah. Ask the congregation what freedom means to them. Include a reference to the United Nations Charter, which includes freedom of speech, thought, beliefs and movement.

Call to Worship

Let the truth of God dawn on our lives.
Let the love of God fill our hearts.
Let the freedom of God liberate our spirits.
God of truth, love and freedom, we worship you.

Prayer of Confession

Voice 1:   Creator God, you made us to fly like eagles and soar above the heavens, to see the world in its beauty and glory. Forgive us for so often living life as if we are trapped in a cage and wanting to look no further than our own tiny existence.
Gentle God, you tenderly caress us when our hearts have been wounded, and soothe our pain when our feelings have been hurt. Forgive us when we try to get our own back and cannot let go of our thirst for revenge.
Merciful God, with loving kindness you look into our eyes when they are full of tears and sadness, when we cannot cope with what has happened to us, when feelings of rejection and loneliness overwhelm us.

Forgive us when bitterness gets the better of us and we lash out at those whom we love and who care for us.

Voice 2:   Merciful and gentle God, creator of us all,
you have made us in your image.
You want us to be whole people, living in peace.
You give us your love and truth to set us free from all bitterness, hatred, thoughts of revenge and smallness of mind.
May we live to your honour and glory through the grace of Jesus Christ. **Amen**

Prayers of Intercession

Let us pray for the oppressed people of the world, for the freedom they seek and the justice which is rightly theirs. For freedom:
– to live in a relationship of trust and peace;
– to worship and believe according to their own consciences;
– to protest against evil and wrong-doing;
– to stand for that which is right and lovely;
– to earn a just and honest living.

So we name before you . . .

These prayers we offer in the name of Christ who was oppressed, suffered and died an unjust death on a cross, but whose resurrection brings hope for all humankind. **Amen**

Offering Prayer

Loving God, you have given us so many things.
Through your Son we possess life and all that is good and true.
We offer these gifts with the prayer that they may be used to offer that life to all who seek it. **Amen**

Dismissal

Go and live in the strength and grace of the Holy Spirit. You have been set free to serve one another – do so with joy, knowing that you do God's will. **Amen**

16th Sunday after Pentecost

Presentation

Sheep and shepherds dominate the readings. In Jesus' days the shepherd led from the front and the sheep followed. It was the shepherd's voice which called the sheep together, otherwise they would wander off and get lost.

Either record some famous voices or ask members of the congregation to sit with their eyes closed while someone speaks – can they identify the speaker? In life which voices do we listen to – parents, politicians, church leaders, others? Do we take any notice? How do we know which voice to follow?

Call to Worship

We are joined to God in an eternal covenant, sealed by his Son.
Let us worship God, whose promises last for ever.

Meditation

Voices, voices, I am surrounded by voices!
Do this, come here, go there, believe this, buy the best, listen to me, give it to me, be quiet!
I am surrounded by voices.
Some want my money, others my time.
Some bring me to tears.
I hear the cry of hungry children;
  the voice of a stranger in the refugee camp;
  the wails of the bereaved as they bury their dead;
  all victims of war and of the world's inhumanity.
I hear the voice of the beggar sitting in the street;
  the cry of the disturbed mind;
  the knock of the lonely person at my door;
  all demanding my attention and help.
All these voices.
They harass me, haunt me.
Tell them to be quiet, tell them to go away.
Let me close my curtains and hide in my room.
Let me live in peace, away from it all.
Yet, as I shut out the world, so, Lord, I shut out you.

For you are the refugee, the victim, the prisoner, the child, the
one who needs me.
You cry out in despair for help.
You call my name to go out and meet you,
to take the risk of following you wherever you may lead,
to find you in the midst of human life.
Help me, Lord, to listen to the voices,
to listen and not to be afraid,
to listen to you speaking from the heart of humanity.
And having listened, help me to speak and act for you.

Prayer of Petition

L: Friendly Shepherd:
R: **Guide us in the ways of peace**.
L: Loving Shepherd:
R: **Hold us in the crook of your arm**.
L: Loyal Shepherd:
R: **Search for us when we go astray**.
L: Suffering Shepherd:
R: **Stand by us in our hour of need**.
L: Gentle Shepherd:
R: **Comfort us in times of pain.   Amen**

Prayer of Intercession and Petition

Let us pray for all who suffer:
– for the victims of war, famine and disease;   *Silence*
– for the persecuted and those imprisoned for their
  political or religious beliefs;   *Silence*
– for the lonely, in desperate need of friendship;   *Silence*
– for victims of violence and abuse;   *Silence*
– for the bereaved and those who face death;   *Silence*

Lord, if we are the victims of unjust accusations or hurt by the
wrong-doing of others, help us, by our forgiveness, to bear
witness to the suffering love of Jesus Christ, remembering that he
died for all and lives for ever more.   **Amen**

17th Sunday after Pentecost

II Chron. 7.11–16
Eph. 3.14–21
John 10.22–30

Presentation

Knowing how to listen is an important gift. Only when we have listened and understood can we act to meet someone's needs. God promises to listen to the prayers of his people, and to act upon them. When we listen to one another communication becomes that much easier. Use listening aids as a visual display – telephone, hearing aid etc. Play a version of 'Chinese Whispers' or do a role play in which two people talk but do not listen to each other. The John reading can have added effect if the question in verse 24b is asked by a group in the congregation.

Call to Worship

L: Let us worship the Father, from whom every family in
   heaven and on earth takes its name:
R: **He pays attention with open ears and eyes**.
L: Let us worship God with thanksgiving:
R: **He knows our inmost thoughts**.
L: Let us bring to God the needs of the world:
R: **He is ready and willing to act, to bring justice
   and love to all in need**.
L: Let us worship the one God through Jesus Christ the
   Son and by the power of the Holy Spirit.

Prayer of Praise

Praise to God who listens to his creation.
Praise to God who hears the cries of the poor.
Praise to God who speaks words of justice and mercy.
Praise to God who sent Jesus to be our brother.
Praise to God who acts like a mother.
Praise to God who gives us everlasting love.
Praise to God who lives in our hearts and minds.
Praise to the living God, the merciful and compassionate, the
forgiver of sins, the supporter of the weak, the defender of the
oppressed, Father and Mother of us all.
Praise to the living God, today and forever.   **Amen**

Prayer of Petition

Loving God,
   help us to respond when others tell us of their needs:
– open our eyes to see their anguish;
– open our ears to hear their fear;
– open our hearts to feel their pain;
– open our minds to the thoughts they express;
– open our hands to feel their grasp.

Loving God, you listened and saw and felt and heard and knew
the needs of the world, then you acted by sending your Son as
the Saviour. By your Spirit help us to respond to others with his
love and care.
May we give and give again, without counting the cost,
May we strive for justice and not heed our own hurt,
May we toil and never rest until your work is done,
May we go the extra mile and not ask for any reward, except to
know we are doing your will.
Now to him who, by the power of the Spirit, is able to work in us
immeasurably more than we can ask or think, to him be glory in
the church and in Christ Jesus from generation to generation for
evermore.   **Amen**

Offering Prayer

This place is the house of sacrifice.
Lord, as we offer our gifts,
we ask that you will open your hands to receive them,
                    open your ears to hear our praise,
                    open your heart to accept our love,
                    open our lives to know your power.
Through Jesus Christ, who is one with you.   **Amen**

Dismissal

May you know the length, breadth, height and depth of Christ's
love, and be filled with the very fullness of God.
May the Spirit of Christ live in your hearts by faith.
Glory be to God, the Father, the Son and the Holy Spirit, from
generation to generation for evermore!   **Amen**

18th Sunday after Pentecost

Presentation

In today's lections 'wisdom' and 'understanding' are closely linked,
Proverbs affirms the wisdom of God in creation, and John stresses
the importance of understanding the significance of Jesus' deeds,
Paul recognizes the depth of 'the wealth and the wisdom and the
knowledge of God'.

    Focus on the other theme in Proverbs, the supreme value of
wisdom in human life. Before reading Proverbs give a list of great
things – i.e. gold, jewels, riches, long life, honour, and wisdom and
ask the congregation which is their *first choice.*

Call to Worship

Glory to the all-wise God, through whom all things exist.
Glory to the Creator,
    whose wisdom laid the world's foundations.
Glory to the Son,
    whose wise words and deeds revealed the Father.
Worship God, whose love and truth is wisdom for all.

Prayer of Praise

Eternal God, the source of all wisdom and understanding, you
chose to come to earth, born as a baby, born not to people of
power and influence but to a humble woman and a working man,
in a borrowed room on a bed of straw, and therefore we praise
you, we worship and adore you.

Loving God, Mother and Father of the earth, the world needs
your gentle touch and tender caress to heal its bitterness, forgive
its sin and make it whole once more.
By your wisdom the world was created,
by your wisdom it will be redeemed,
and therefore we praise you, we worship and adore you.

Faithful God, bearer of our pain, carer for the sick,
you stand by all who suffer and struggle through life.
Your compassionate strength upholds the weak and challenges
the powerful. Give us wisdom and understanding of your will for

humankind, so that we may speak and act in the name of Christ,
through whose name we praise you, we worship and adore
you.   **Amen**

Prayer of Confession

When we treasure possessions more than thoughts;
L: Lord: R: **Forgive us**.
When we despise the wisdom of others;
L: Lord: R: **Forgive us**.
When we forget all we have learned of your ways;
L: Lord: R: **Forgive us**.
When we abuse the wisdom you have given us.
L: Lord: R: **Forgive us**.
In your wisdom and mercy you forgive us through your Son.
Thanks be to you, O Lord.   **Amen**

Prayer of Intercession

Let us pray for Wisdom to prevail in the world:
L: Where there is hatred: R: **Let there be love**.
L: Where there is unrest: R: **Let there be peace**.
L: Where there is poverty: R: **Let there be plenty**.
L: Where there is pain: R: **Let there be joy**.
L: Where there is despair: R: **Let there be hope**.
L: Where there is emptiness: R: **Let there be fulfillment**.

Help us, God the Holy Spirit, bringer of wisdom to those who
seek God's way, to use all your gifts in the service of humanity.
And may all who see our good deeds have the wisdom to
recognize your hand at work, respond in faith and come to praise
your name.   **Amen**

Dismissal

On all your journeys take with you the wealth,
wisdom and knowledge of God. May God give you
comfort for today and strength for tomorrow,
courage in the face of adversity and joy in the face of grief.
Go with God, for God is with you for all time.   **Amen**

19th Sunday after Pentecost

Presentation

An evident theme is 'dying and rising again'. In Daniel God promises eternal life to faithful Israelites at the End. The raising of Lazarus, according to John, will show God's glory and encourage the disciples to believe. And Paul affirms the possibility of a life beyond death which is more than a disembodied 'immortality of the soul'. Every-day life, however, offers experiences which shed light on 'death and resurrection'. Ask the congregation to share experiences of redun-dancy and a new career, losing a friend and making up, and other similar examples they can think of. In the John reading a number of people can take the different roles.

   Also see next week.

Call to Worship

God, you are the source of our lives on earth,
you are the source of our lives in Christ.
In faith we gather in your name, to worship you,
Lord of all life, physical and spiritual.

Offering Prayer

Lord, you give us so many good things; you have given us life,
and life eternal; use all that we have and are so that others may
enjoy abundant life in you.   **Amen**

Prayers of Intercession   *Light a candle after each bidding as a sign of God giving new life in place of death*

Let us pray for people whose lives hover between life and death.
For those:
– who are critically ill;
– who wait for life-saving operations;
– who are injured through an accident;
– who hunger and thirst;
– who are wounded in war;
– who find life unbearable and long for death.

Lord, we pray for . . .
May they know that this life is not the end, and that the life to be found in you is stronger than death. May they find healing and hope, strength and courage, peace and comfort even in the midst of pain and distress.

Let us pray for those who have been bereaved. For:
- parents mourning the death of young children;
- children confused and distressed by the loss of a
  parent;
- families relieved that the suffering of elderly
  relatives is at an end;
- widows and widowers left with a void no one else seems
  able to fill.

Lord, we pray for . . .
May they know that you bring new life and new hope to shattered lives, that your peace is more than the world can give and that your love can comfort their sorrow.

Let us pray for those who risk death because of their beliefs. For:
- people of faith who struggle for truth and justice;
- those who face persecution, imprisonment and torture
  for their ideals;
- all who, by their example, challenge our conscience.

Lord, we pray for . . .
May they know your strength and find courage to hold fast to the truth. May they reveal your way and show those who hold them captive the injustice of their ways and a better way of life, with justice for all.

Through him who is the Resurrection and the Life, who suffers still for those who suffer and mourns with those who mourn, Jesus Christ our Lord and Saviour.   **Amen**

Dismissal

God live in you his risen life,
this day and for ever more.

20th Sunday after Pentecost

Job 42.1–6
Phil. 1.12–30
John 11.28–44

Presentation

To hear about God from others is helpful but to see God for ourselves gives life an entirely new quality. We can speak of him with a new confidence and, discerning his activity in the world, can be strengthened in our work and witness. As an aid to worship use material from nature and the creative arts in which we can 'see' God. Ask members of the congregation to speak of their activities (e.g. preaching, pastoral visiting, smiling) through which, they believe, God is revealed. See last week for other prayers.

Call of Worship

Let us worship the living God revealed in Jesus Christ
    and made known to us through the Holy Spirit.
Let us worship the living God who gives us eyes to see
    and ears to hear and hearts to love.

Prayer of Praise

Living God, we praise you for all that reveals you at work in the world.
    For all that is beautiful and brings us joy;
    trees and flowers, birds and animals,
    rivers and seas,
    mountains and sunshine.

    For people who love us,
    welcoming us into their homes, greeting us when
    we come to worship, comforting us when we are
    sad and visiting us when we are ill.

    For compassion and care, wisdom and insight,
    knowledge and understanding, and for every skill
    and talent through which we can share the
    gospel of Jesus with others.

Living God, help us to look for you in our daily lives, wherever
we go and whatever we do. Help us to see you in the ordinary as
well as the special, in people as well as events. Surprise us when

we least expect you and make yourself known to us in times of need.
Living God, we give you our thanks and praise.   **Amen**

Prayer of Confession *Based on John 11.21, 32*

'Lord, if you had been here my brother would not have died.'

Lord, we ask your forgiveness when we doubt you.
When things do not go as we want them to,
it is you we blame, asking why and why not.
When we do not recognize you with us,
we say you have forgotten us.
When you do not answer our prayers as we wish,
we accuse you of being fickle or deaf to our pleas.
But the fault is ours.
It is our faith which is lacking.
Lord, forgive us, and help us always to trust you.   **Amen**

Prayer of Petition

L: Lord, you opened the eyes of a blind man. Open our eyes to
　　see you, to recognize the needs of others:
R: **So that we may respond in love**.

L: Lord, you raised Lazarus from the dead.
　　Lift us to new life, fill us with new hope:
R: **So that we may respond in love**.

L: Lord, you changed the life of Paul.
　　Fill our hearts and minds with the good news of Christ:
R: **So that we may respond in love**.

Dismissal

Go out into the world with the risen Christ;
　　meet his need in your neighbour,
　　take his light into dark places.
Go out into the world with Christ and live!

21st Sunday after Pentecost

Presentation

Today's readings focus on a promise, a covenant and a plan. Jephthah's promise to God produced a tragedy; Jesus' death established a new covenant between God and humankind; and the Sanhedrin planned, successfully, to kill Jesus. There are incidental lessons to be learned, e.g. about not making promises rashly and about how people can say more than they realize. But a single focus on 'promise' will be helpful. Beginning from a bank note's 'I promise to pay the bearer on demand'!, encourage the congregation to recall vows and promises they have made – New Year resolutions, marriage vows, baptismal promises, confirmation vows – and use symbols of promise, e.g. a rainbow and a cross, as visual aids to worship.

Call to Worship

The God we worship today has promised that he will never leave us nor forsake us but be present and remain faithful through all ages.
Let us praise and adore, and give God the glory.

Prayer of Confession

Faithful and loving God,
we praise and thank you for your consistent love;
– love which formed the world and the human race,
– love which sent Jesus Christ to be our Saviour,
– love which, despite our unfaithfulness, will never end.

Voice 1:   For not keeping the promises we make to one another, Lord: **Forgive us**.

Voice 2:   For putting ourselves first when others are in need, Lord: **Forgive us**.

Voice 1:   For falling out with friends when we don't get our own way, Lord: **Forgive us**.

Voice 2:   For not always telling the truth and hoping to get away with it, Lord: **Forgive us**.

You know us, God of love, better than we know ourselves.
You know that we are proud, selfish and wilful, yet you remain
faithful to us.
And we are grateful, for we cannot live without you.
We know you forgive those who are sorry and wish to make
amends. We ask for your forgiveness now, assured of your love.
Help us through your grace and the strength of your Spirit, to
live according to your way of love.
In the name of Jesus, our Saviour.   **Amen**

A Meditation

It is easy to remind others of what they promised:
   'You said you would do the ironing, but it isn't finished!'
   'You said you would visit Grandma, but you haven't been!'
   'You said you would clean the chapel, but it's still untidy!'
   'You said you would . . ., but you didn't!'
It is even easier to forget that we too fail to keep our word and
make excuses for not keeping our promises.

Yet sometimes it is more serious than that.
I promised to follow you, Lord, but it's a struggle.
When I said 'yes' to you,
I didn't realize that discipleship could involve:
– visiting the sick and comforting the suffering;
– collecting for charities door-to-door;
– writing to the prisoner;
– protesting about injustice;
– being a friend to my next-door-neighbour.
When I said 'yes' to you,
I forgot that with your help what I do and say can reveal your
presence in the world, so that others can know your love.

Lord, you have said 'yes' to me.
You accept me as I am, and call me to change.
You have put your life in me.
By the sign of the cross you have claimed me to be your own.
So I am yours and you are mine.
May it be so for ever and ever.

22nd Sunday after Pentecost

II Sam. 23.13–17
Acts 6.1–7
John 13.12–30

Presentation

Serving others is central to discipleship. As today's readings tell us, it can involve taking risks, sharing in pastoral ministry, serving others, and being prepared to be let down. And, in each case our motivation should be a genuine interest in other people.

Discover the church's local expression of such service, displaying the work which is done like fruit on a tree, and inviting the congregation to indicate their contributions (e.g. charitable work, helping a neighbour, etc.) on cards which are collected and dedicated with the offering.

Call to Worship

Remembering all that we have said and done during the past week, we meet to worship God who has sustained us.
Looking forward to the challenges of the coming week, we meet to worship God who will strengthen us.
To hear again the call to discipleship and find the power of the Spirit to fulfil it,
we meet to worship God and renew our faith.

A Framework for an Intercessory Prayer

L: May they know the presence of your Spirit:
R: **As they seek to serve you in the world**.

Let us pray for all who seek to serve other people,
in the name of Christ the Preacher, for:
– *mention ministers, local preachers, missionaries, evangelists, 'prophets in their own land'.*

in the name of Christ the Healer, for:
– *mention health workers, counsellors, chaplains, charity workers, pastoral visitors.*

in the name of Christ the Teacher, for:
– *mention teachers and lecturers, youth workers, Junior Church leaders, Brigade officers.*

Jesus Christ, servant of the servants, you call us to a life of service. Give us the humility to take up a bowl and towel and wash the feet of all in need.
Help us, by your Spirit, to live out the gospel as we serve you in the world. **Amen**

Prayer of Petition

The soldiers took the risk of fetching water for David:
   – they did something dangerous for the one they served.
The early church took the risk of appointing Stephen and six others to look after the money and distribute charity:
   – they did something new and worthwhile.
Jesus took the risk of serving his followers by humbly washing their feet:
   – he did something unusual but profound.

Servant God, in serving others you call us to take risks with our time, talents, money, buildings, energy.
You challenge us to risk our very selves.
You encourage us to try new things and stop playing safe,
   to move out from our predictable ways
   and to be bold in our actions.
You teach us to be the church in the world,
not the church behind closed doors.

Servant God,
help us to take our courage in both hands and to respond in faith to your call to go with you into the unknown,
to risk failure in order to succeed in spreading your love,
and to discover afresh the joy of your salvation. **Amen**

Blessing and Dismissal

May God bless you as you serve others and fill you with the Spirit of love. Go and serve, for the joy of knowing that you serve your Lord and Master, Jesus Christ. **Amen**

Last Sunday after Pentecost

Presentation

*The readings all look ahead: Jeremiah to a time beyond the exile;
Paul to a heavenly prize; Jesus to a time when the disciples will have
to continue his mission without his physical presence. But in each
case the future is related to a present attitude or activity.*

*What is the congregation looking forward to, both as individuals
and as the church? What planning needs to take place? What have
Christians to say about facing the future? Using Paul's image of sport
or the arts, music, or science, how does preparation in the present
affect results in the future?*

Jeremiah 29.12 could be used as a response for prayers.

Call to Worship

Come and worship the living God;
- who loved us before the world began,
- who made himself known to us through Jesus,
- who listens to our prayers,
- who will be found by all who seek in faith.
Let us worship our wonderful God.

Prayer of Welcome

Lord, you met people as they were, and loved them equally.
May we welcome the stranger with open acceptance,
   welcome the young couple looking for a home,
   welcome the new baby with cries of delight,
   welcome the older person with respect for their
     experience,
   welcome all who are different from us.
In welcoming them, may we welcome you, and recognize that
you are among them, so that we can receive what they have to
offer us.
May we all be as one, as we welcome you into our lives.
  Amen

Meditation on the 'Race of life'   (*Phil. 3.14*)

Here I am, Lord,
waiting for the off.
Listening for the starter to say 'Ready, steady, go!'
Yet the race is already being run
and this is just a lap on the way.
And there, in the distance, I can see the finishing line,
the place I am aiming for,
the goal of all my efforts.
A lot of effort is already behind me.
I've done the practice
– trained hard so that I can give my best.
Yet the tape, the end, seems so far away.
Will I manage it, or stumble and fall,
or give up through sheer exhaustion.
Will I get the prize?
No, not first, second, or third but the prize of completing the
race, of endurance, of life, knowing that I have taken part and
faithfully given all.

Lord, help me to run the best race I have ever run.
At this moment, as I listen for the starting gun,
give me the courage and love to keep the faith,
taking life's hurdles in my stride
and let me know that you are coaching me and pacing me.
Here I am, Lord, waiting,
surrounded by all those who have run the race before me and
those who are running it with me.
Encourage me when the going gets tough.
Lift me up when the going is rough.
Keep my eyes fixed on the finishing line.
Now I know that I can make it and that with you I will not fall.
With your hand to guide me and love to keep me, I will gain the
heavenly prize and receive a victor's crown.

Dismissal

Go, and be imitators of Christ.
Go, and feed the world with God's love.
Go, and let the Holy Spirit be your companion and guide.
Go, and give glory to God who goes with you.

Church Anniversary

Presentation

To be a member of Christ's flock is cause enough for celebration, and today is also this church's birthday. Decorate the church as for a birthday, with streamers, balloons, etc. Strike a joyful note.

Call to Worship

'I was glad when they said to me
"Let us go to the house of the Lord" '
On this, our church's birthday
let us worship God with gladness and joy.

Prayer

God, our heavenly Father,
    we come together in your church,
    as members of your family
    who are seeking to follow
    the example of Jesus Christ,
    your only Son.

God of joy and friendship,
    we come together in your church
    to celebrate your love for us
    and our love for one another.

God of past and present and future,
    we come together in your church
    gratefully to remember the past;
    truly to live in the present;
    to work hopefully for the future.

God of grace and generosity,
    we come together in your church
    to thank you in our worship
    for the gift of your Son;
    for the riches of your love;
    for the fullness of Christian life.

God of forgiveness and mercy,
   we confess that we have forgotten:
     – to be loving;
     – to be joyful;
     – to be trusting;
     – to be thankful;
   and we come together in your church
   to ask for a new beginning
   on our journey of faith.

We make our prayers
   in the name of the founder of our faith,
   our Lord and Saviour, Jesus Christ.　**Amen**

Prayer of Dedication

Lord, you call us to be your disciples
   to follow you;
   to bring your love to those
     among whom we live and work;
   to discover their needs
   and seek to meet them.

Lord, you call us to be your disciples
   to turn the whole world upside down;
   to bring your love
   to the poor,
   to the oppressed,
   to victims of injustice,
   and to all who suffer.

Lord, at this church anniversary
we dedicate ourselves to you.
In the strength of your Holy Spirit,
may we be partners with you,
in bringing your transforming love to all creation.　**Amen**

YEAR D   Deut. 26.1–11 *or* Lev. 19.9–18
Harvest Festival   II Cor. 9.6–15
                                     John 12.23–28

Presentation

*Each reading is about 'thanks' and 'giving'. Divide the service into
two clear sections – 'thanks' for the gifts of harvest, 'giving' for the
needs of others. Make it clear that the 'giving' in question is not out of
guilt but in response to the generosity of God to us.*

*The two sections could be identified by visual signals, posters,
changing the position of leading the service, etc.*

Call to Worship

Read Deut. 26.1–4. Holding up a harvest basket say:
We acknowledge this day that the Lord has provided food for our
needs.
The produce of land and sea is a gift for our enjoyment.
Thanks be to God for the bountiful harvest we have received.
Set the basket down on the communion table.

Prayer of Thanksgiving   *Collect ideas from the congregation*

For apples, beans and carrots . . .
   for watermelons, yams and zucchinis.
L: For the gifts of God: R: **We give our thanks**.

For salt, coal and iron . . .
   for water, oil and wind.
L: For the gifts of God: R: **We give our thanks**.

For cotton, silk, leather and wool . . .
   for nylon, polythene, plastic and acrylic
L: For the gifts of God: R: **We give our thanks**.

God, giver of all that is good,
for your harvest we thank you.   **Amen**

Offering Prayer *Read Lev. 19.9–10*

Holding the offering plate(s), as above, say:
We acknowledge this day that God has provided for us and that
we have enough to help the poor and the stranger.
Accept, Lord, these gifts in gratitude for your generous love.
Set the plate down on the communion table.

Prayer of Dedication

Lord, we have enough and to spare:
   ample food; warm, attractive clothes;
   dry, comfortable homes.
L: In thanksgiving:
R: **We pledge ourselves to be good stewards of all your gifts**.

Lord, we have been richly blessed:
   with caring relatives and friends;
   with the fellowship of brothers and sisters in Christ;
   with your love throughout our lives.
L: In thanksgiving:
R: **We pledge ourselves to be good stewards of all your gifts**.

Lord, we are supported and enriched:
   by good schools and colleges;
   by skilled doctors and fine hospitals;
   by an affluent society.
L: In thanksgiving:
R: **We pledge ourselves to be good stewards of all your gifts**.

Help us, Lord, always to remember your generous love,
   to find increasing joy in your service,
   and to give as you have given to us.
In the name of Jesus,   **Amen**

Dismissal   (*Based on II Cor. 9.6–8*)

'Sow sparingly, and you will reap sparingly;
sow bountifully, and you will reap bountifully.'
Go and sow God's love and peace, and you will harvest love and
peace in abundance, for 'God loves a cheerful giver.'

Appendix

For users of other Lectionaries

The following pages contain a biblical index, cross-references from ASB to JLG2 and a theme index.

Each of these will suggest suitable material for users of other lectionaries (or no set lectionary at all). Not every set of readings or all the themes in the ASB are covered by these two years of JLG2 but, where possible, material is suggested which might be suitable.

Index of Biblical Passages

Index of Themes

(Titles in brackets are themes listed in ASB
with suitable Sundays from JLG2 suggested)

Theme	Sunday	Year	Theme	Sunday	Year
Abraham, faith of	7C	D	Creation (Job)	9C	C
Abraham, promise to	7C	C	Death & resurrection	2E,P19	D
Acceptance by God	P13	D	Discipleship	P15	C
Acceptance of			Emmaus Road	E1	C
others	P5	C	(Endurance	P9	C)
Adoration	3E, E3	D	Faith	5E	C
Advent Hope	4C	C		E1	D
(Annunciation	1C	C & D)	Faithfulness	3E	C
Ascension	E6	C	Fall	8C	D
Authority	P22	C	(First Disciples	Ep2	D)
(Baptism of Jesus	Ep1	C & D)	Following	5E	D
Bible	3C	C & D	Food	7E	D
Bread of Life	E3	C	(Forerunner	2C	D)
	P10	D	Freedom	Ep6	C
Call of God	P9	C		P15	D
(Charge to Peter	E2	D)		P19	C
Christ the Healer	5E	D	(Freedom of the		
Christ the King	C1	D	Sons of God	E4	C)
Christ the Messiah	4E	C	(Fruit of the Spirit	E4	D)
Christ the Teacher	9E	C	Future hope	E6	C
(Christ the Friend			Gifts (Wise Men's)	C1	C
of Sinners	P19	D	Glory of God	3E	C
	P6	D	Good News	Ep1	C
	P13	D)	God's care	7E	C
Christian clothing	P16	C	God's providence	7E	D
(Christian Hope	E2	D)	(Going to the Father	E5	D)
Christian life	P9	D	Growth	C2	D
Christian service	P22	D	Guidance	Ep3	C
Church	Ep4	C	Healing	8E	C
	Ch Ann	C & D	Healing, touch	P3	D
Church, worship	Ep4	D	Holiness	Ep6, E4	D
(Church's Mission	4E	C	(Holy Family	C2	D)
	P4	C)	Holy Spirit	Pent	C & D
(Citizens of Heaven	PLast	D)	Hope	P6	C
(Confidence in Christ	P3	C)		P5	D
(Conflict	5E, 6E	C)	Humility	P14	C
Covenant	P21	C	Incarnation	C & C2	C)
Creation (Genesis)	9C	D	Jesus, Son of God	Ep1	D

Index of Themes